Research, Teaching, and Learning with the Piaget Model

Research, Teaching, and Learning with the Piaget Model

by
John W. Renner
Donald G. Stafford
Anton E. Lawson
Joe W. McKinnon
F. Elizabeth Friot
Donald H. Kellogg

University of Oklahoma Press : Norman

By John W. Renner

Physics for Today (filmstrip series, Chicago, 1958)
Experiments and Exercises in Physics (Philadelphia, 1961)
Mechanics (filmstrip series, with Duane Courter, New York, 1962)
Involving the Child with Science (cassett series, Hollywood, 1971)
Wings for a Dinosaur: An Anthology on Science Education (Oklahoma City, 1972)
Guiding Learning in the Elementary School (with G. Shepherd and R. Bibens, New York, 1973)
Guiding Learning in the Secondary School (with G. Shepherd and R. Bibens, New York, 1972)
Teaching Science in the Secondary School (with G. Shepherd and R. Bibens, New York, 1973)
Teaching Science in the Elementary School, Second Edition (with Don G. Stafford and W. B. Ragan, New York, 1973)
Physical Science: Inquiry and Investigation (with Donald G. Stafford, Beverly Hills, 1976)
Investigation in Physics (with H. B. Packard, Chicago, 1974)
Research, Teaching, and Learning with the Piaget Model (with Donald G. Stafford, Anton E. Lawson, Joe W. McKinnon, F. Elizabeth Friot, and Donald H. Kellogg, Norman, 1976)

Also by Donald G. Stafford

Teaching Science in the Elemtary School (New York, 1973)
Teaching Science in the Secondary School (New York, 1973)
Physical Science: Inquiry and Investigation (with John W. Renner, Beverly Hills, 1976)

Library of Congress Cataloging in Publication Data
Main entry under title:

Research, teaching, and learning with the Piaget model.

Includes bibliographical references.
1. Cognition (Child psychology) 2. Piaget, Jean, 1861– 3. Learning, Psychology of. I. Renner, John Wilson, 1924–
BF723.C5R47   370.15'2   75–17800
ISBN 0–8061–1313–8

Preface

We believe that one of the fundamental educational needs is truly basic research at the classroom level on how learners of all ages learn and what they can learn. Only if that information is available can a determination be made whether or not the objectives of education are being achieved. When schools evaluate them selves upon the achievement of their objectives, *true educational accountability is being exercised.*

In the fall of 1968 we began the research described in this book; that research was completed in 1973. Areas of research were selected that we felt would have the greatest impact upon how a teacher and a learner interact. Jean Piaget's concept of conservation reasoning seemed to us to be the starting point for finding out the interaction that exists between curriculum and intellectual development. We began there.

Our work in the area of conservation reasoning has been criticized because, our critics say, we are interested in leading children to exercise conservation reasoning at younger and younger ages. Not so! What we are interested in finding out is whether the curricula that are found in schools and that accurately portray the discipline will allow children to move through the intellectual levels described by Piaget as they study the several disciplines from an inquiry frame of reference better than they would from the traditional method which usually employs a textbook. Chapters 2, 5, and 7 are devoted to this concept. Chapter 3 demonstrates the importance of conservation reasoning in one of the basic disciplines, reading.

Chapter 6 represents a unique field of work. We decided to determine where secondary school students fit into the Piagetian model. The data found in that chapter present several factors that we believe need to be considered when curriculum decisions are being made. We also believe that the data shown in Chapter 6 explode several myths about the intellectual superiority of the female to the male. That in turn raises questions regarding why girls seem to "do better" in school than boys.

The first portion of Chapter 6 utilizes a data-treatment technique that delivers an overview of the intellectual-development picture of secondary school students, but, if not carefully studied, can produce some misrepresentations. We have added together scores on six separate Piagetian-type tasks to produce a total score for each individual student interviewed. Even though we weighted the scores on each task, there is no way we can be sure that these weights are precise. The total scores, however, do give a rough picture of the intellectual development of secondary school students. A more precise picture emerges when the performance of the interviewees on each task is considered. That procedure is followed during the latter portion of Chapter 6. Therefore, in order to gain a complete picture of that portion of the research, the entire chapter must be studied before any generalizations can be reached.

Chapter 8 presents a view of the Piagetian intellectual-development model that we have not seen elsewhere. We believe that the procedures utilized in that chapter demonstrate statistical justification for the existence of the concrete and formal operational stages of intellectual development in the Piagetian model. Until this point we had taken the model of Piaget nearly upon faith. We have seen these stages evidenced in children and have made a detailed study of the work of Jean Piaget—those experiences were the reason for our faith. We believe that the statistical analyses in Chapter 8 justify that faith, and, in our opinion, that is important.

The question is often raised whether or not concrete operational thinkers can operate intellectually with formal operational ideas. Chapter 9 presents our research on how concrete and formal thinkers react to formal and concrete items written to test the comprehension of concepts in biology, chemistry, and physics that have supposedly been taught.

We believe the data and interpretations found in this book will lead to reflection upon the job of teaching in a different way. That was our experience.

Norman, Oklahoma

John W. Renner
Donald G. Stafford
Anton E. Lawson
Joe W. McKinnon
F. Elizabeth Friot
Donald H. Kellogg

Contents

Illustrations

Figures

Research, Teaching, and Learning with the Piaget Model

1. Learning and Piaget

John W. Renner

Any institution that does not have a thorough understanding
of its purposes will eventually be destroyed or destroy itself.
Our educational system is no exception, and that system has
been delineating its purposes for over 350 years. American
schools were established primarily to teach reading so that
children could read the Bible. Educational programs overtly
aimed at citizenship, life adjustment, basic education (whatever that is), vocational education, the air age, the nuclear age,
and the space age have found their way into the curricula of
secondary and elementary schools. But every program from
reading the Bible to space-age education has been based upon
the assumption that there are certain pieces of information,
facts, skills, and attitudes that must be presented to the learner.
Whether or not that assumption has merit and validity is

Much of the material in this chapter was adapted with permission
from John W. Renner, Robert F. Bibens, and Gene D. Shepherd, *Guiding
Learning in the Secondary School* (New York, Harper and Row, 1972)
Chap. 4.

debatable. The general assumption was also made that presenting the learner the material and involving him with it would also teach him to think. Because of that assumption such subjects as Greek, Latin, Euclidean geometry, and many others have been kept in the curricula for years, particularly in the secondary schools. Intellectual development, therefore, was considered to be a concomitant outcome.

Our hypothesis is that the exact reverse is probably true— that is, that if educational programs are overtly designed to foster intellectual development, the understanding of the material from any discipline that "must" be taught will be the concomitant outcome. We believe that evidence exists to support our hypothesis and that that evidence will be found in this volume. Obviously, to test our hypothesis, school programs and procedures will have to be arranged much differently from their present structure. Some of those new curricular arrangements and procedures are discussed in the Chapter 10.

Before rearranging the educational system to accomplish this goal, two questions must be asked: (1) What should be the purpose of such an educational institution? and (2) How will teachers, administrators, and parents know when intellectual development has been accomplished?

The answer to the first question is obvious: to lead children toward intellectual development, or the development of the ability to think was stated in 1961 by the Educational Policies Commission in its essay "The Central Purpose of American Education." The commission stated that any person who had developed the essence of thinking ability could use the rational powers of recalling, imagining, comparing, evaluating, classifying, generalizing, analyzing, synthesizing, deducing, and inferring. Here, then, is a purpose to which schools can subscribe and produce programs that will lead children to achieve. Furthermore, this purpose can be thoroughly understood by those implementing it— by teachers and administrators. That purpose will also govern every act of interaction among children, content, and teachers as well as content selection. In other words, the development of the ability to think will truly become *central* to the activities of the school.

The answer to the second question represents a task to which Jean Piaget has dedicated his life and which is the subject of this book. When you have read the book, the intellectual-development model of Jean Piaget will be available to you to use in determining what progress is being made in leading children toward intellectual development.

A school, then, that is concerned with intellectual development has a central, unifying purpose—the development of the ability to think—toward which the learning within it is directed. A way of determining the progress that has been made is represented by the intellectual-development model of Piaget. Intellectual development, of course, represents what we believe is the true nature of learning. Thus, before we begin to examine the Piagetian model, learning as it is presently viewed in the schools and learning as the Piagetian model demands that it be viewed need to be examined.

The tradition of our schools has been that all learners are directed toward the same objectives and that the teacher can, through testing, determine how much progress is made. The greater the progress made by the learner the higher the grade he receives. That system makes several assumptions, such as that all learners are equally motivated to achieve the objectives, the objectives are equally important and relevant for every learner, the teacher communicates equally effectively with each child, and all learners have had the same kinds of experience, which makes them all begin the learning on an equal footing. Although the foregoing assumptions are made when a content-centered course is taught, *none of them is valid*. Examine, for example, the last assumption. If all learners do not have identical backgrounds and if each is graded on the progress made toward a rigid set of course objectives, those children bringing the richest backgrounds of experience into the course will receive the best grades. In that case not only are grades not assigned just on the basis of the learning accomplished in the course but also they are a function of all of the previous experience a learner has had. For a teacher to assign grades on the basis of how far the learners have progressed toward the course objectives and to call those grades a measure of the achievement made in that class is an obvious absurdity. If grades are to be assigned—and such a procedure is difficult to defend if the development of the ability to think is the central purpose of education—they must be awarded on the basis of how effectively the learner applied himself to the task of learning and not how much information, or "knowledge," he could cram into his head in preparation for an examination. Albert Szen-Györgi states his position thus: "Books are there to keep the knowledge in while we use our heads for something better."[1] That something better is, of course, the ability to think.

Society has—and justifiably so—certain content it wishes taught, with which schools must have students interact in order to develop the ability to think. Grades must be assigned on the students' success in developing the ability to think with that content. The intellectual-development model of Piaget is useful to schools in demonstrating this true accountability with respect to learning. The remainder of this book is devoted to learning and our research about it. Before we begin, you need to know precisely where you are, so take a few minutes and write down your present understanding of what the learning process is all about.

Interaction and Structure

Development has been thought of traditionally as the sum of all of a person's discrete learning experiences. Jean Piaget expresses a different belief "Development is the essential process and each element of learning occurs as a function of total development, rather than being an element which explains

[1]Albert Szent-Györgi, "Teaching and the Expanding Knowledge," *Science*, December, 1964, pp. 1278–79.

development."[2] In other words (although improving Piaget's statement is difficult), the development that a learner undergoes explains what he can learn rather than that the learning explains and accounts for his development.

If we assume that the material to be learned is clearly within the development pattern of the learners (and how that determination is made will be discussed later), how do they learn and gain knowledge about the material? Piaget's basic hypothesis about learning is that to know something is to act upon it and/or interact with it. Knowing an object, event, or situation is not simply looking at it and making a mental copy of it. Suppose, for example, that you wished to teach Newton's first law of motion, which is that moving objects will continue moving in a straight line, and that objects at rest will remain at rest unless the objects in both cases are acted upon by some force coming from outside the objects. A learner can make a mental copy of this particular law and make perfect scores on any examination he is given, but he will soon forget it. In addition, when he meets the law or its results, he will not be able to function with it because he has no mental *structure* he can use in categorizing and assigning meaning to the information he receives. If, however, he has a learning experience during which he acts upon moving and resting objects and interacts with the same kinds of objects, he will begin to build mental structures about them. When he next encounters a situation that involves moving bodies, he has a structure to use in processing the information. Whether or not the concept of *inertia* is invented for the learners is probably not too important, because the structures necessary to process information about moving and resting bodies have already been built. If, however, the conceptual invention of inertia is made (probably by the teacher), the structure becomes better defined, and discoveries about inertia can go forward.

[2]Jean Piaget, "Development and Learning," *Journal of Research in Science Teaching*, Vol. 2, No. 3 (1964).

The concept of property is learned by experiencing hard, rough, round, thick, and thin and by hearing many other such words that apply to real objects. Photograph by Frederick B. Schmidt.

One of the most widely used concepts in our world is that of *property.* We speak of the properties of objects, material, sounds, events, situations, and all manner of other things. The material demonstrating the concept can be presented to the learners, and they can begin to make mental copies of all kinds of properties. That procedure may produce those who can answer questions about property, but when the "thing" whose properties are to copied is changed, no structure exists that can be used to process the newly received information. Instead of having the learner mentally copy the properties of "things," suppose he begins in the first grade to act upon liquids by mixing them,

interact with the language by producing stories, act upon sand-
paper by feeling it, and in general involving himself with the
property concept. All the while this interaction is going on, the
learner is finding out not so much the specific properties of the
objects studied (that would be copying reality) but something
about the concept of property itself. Property is hard, soft,
sticky, rough, scrunchy, sweet, sour, and so on. Now he is
developing broad mental structures for the property concept,
and, when he meets something in the future relating to property, he has a structure to use in processing those data. This
view of knowing is precisely what Jerome Bruner meant when
he said that "knowing is a process, not a product."[3]

Learning, therefore, proceeds by the interaction of the learner
with something and his assimilation of the results of those interactions and accommodation of those results to his structure
or his structure to the results. The latter act, of course, really
produces a new structure. The materials and/or ideas selected
for the learner to interact with must obviously be at his level of
intellectual development, or structure *cannot* be changed and/or
developed. One cannot, for example, expect a first grader to interact with calculus and construct or build from the interaction.

Cognition

You have probably already recognized that Piaget's learning
model is *cognitive* as opposed to stimulus-response. The field
of developmental learning has had contributions from many
people, but the greatest contributors have no doubt been Piaget
and his long-term associate, Bärbel Inhelder. Piaget explains
the relationship between his learning model and the stimulus-
response model as follows:

Classically, learning is based on the stimulus-response schema. I
think the stimulus-response schema, while I won't say it is false,

---

[3] Jerome Bruner, *Toward a Theory of Instruction*, (Cambridge, Mass.,
Harvard University Press, 1966), 72.

is in any case entirely incapable of explaining cognitive learning. Why? Because when you think of a stimulus-response schema, you think usually that first of all there is a stimulus and then a response is set off by this stimulus. . . . I am convinced that the response was there first . . . . A stimulus is a stimulus only to the extent that it is significant and it becomes significant only to the extent that there is a structure which permits its assimilation, a structure which can integrate this stimulus but which at the same time sets off the response. . . . The stimulus is really a stimulus only when it is assimilated into a structure and it is this structure which sets off the response. Consequently, it is not an exaggeration to say that the response is there first. . . . Once there is a structure the stimulus will set off a response, but only by the intermediary of this structure.[4]

Stimulus response, then, is a viable learning model only because of the existence of cognitive structures and those cognitive structures are constructed by the learner only through the action on and/or the interaction with materials, ideas, objects, and all types of "stuff" found in a learning environment. When a learner is learning by interaction with his environment, he is inquiring. But inquiring will go on in schools only if the teacher believes that inquiry is the classroom procedure to use.

Equilibrium

What has been presented so far about structure development leaves a serious unanswered question: How does a learner deepen his understanding of anything through the cognitive-structure model of learning? Deepened understandings are developed because of the desire of the human organism always to be in a state of mental and physical harmony, or *equilibrium*, with his environment. If an individual is mentally or physically uncomfortable with his situation, he tends to act to reestablish equilibrium.

[4]Piaget, "Development and Learning," *Journal of Research in Science Teaching*, Vol. 2, No. 3 (1964), 176–86.

Now, suppose that a teacher is leading children to develop the concept of property, and the need for the concept of "pentagon" arises. If the children do not have the concept of pentagon in their cognitive structures, this event (or perturbation) produces in many of them a state of disequilibrium. To establish a state of equilibrium again, they and/or the teacher must invent the concept of pentagon.

After the conceptual invention, the learners are back in equilibrium, and they can now employ the concept and make all kinds of discoveries with and about it. But, in making these discoveries, they sharpen their own structures, which have to do, perhaps, with geometrical shape. The learners also begin to find other concepts with which they were in equilibrium before but which are now out of equilibrium with their point of view and interaction with their environment. Here is a new perturbation, and the individual must act to reestablish equilibrium. John L. Phillips, Jr., explains the equilibrium states:

> . . . structures continually move toward a state of equilibrium, and when a state of relative equilibrium has been attained, the structure is sharper, more clearly delineated, than it had been previously. But that very sharpness points up inconsistencies and gaps in the structure that had never been salient before. Each equilibrium state therefore carries with it the seeds of its own destruction.[5]

The teacher, therefore, has the responsibility to provide activities that lead the learner to reach disequilibrium and will produce information that can be interpreted so that equilibrium can be reestablished. This new state of equilibrium has developed for the child a new cognitive structure that is sharper and richer than the one he was disequilibrated from. The learner now views objects, events, and situations from the new structure and sees gaps, inconsistencies, and contradictions that again put him out of equilibrium. Thus, as Phillips says,

[5]John L. Phillips, Jr., *The Origins of Intellect: Piaget's Theory* (San Francisco, W. H. Freeman and Co., 1969), 10.

each new equilibration carries with it the procedure for self-destruction.

Inquiry-centered teaching provides the learner an opportunity to find information and interact with objects, events, and situations as his own. In such a learning plan, the learner constantly faces situations in which he destroys his own structures, builds new ones, and has those destroyed by future findings—that is, of course, equilibrating and disequilibrating himself. In fact, equilibration is the thread that weaves the inquiry-teaching design together, because the purpose of the plan is to involve the learner so completely in the learning that his understandings grow deeper and deeper. But, for a person to deepen an understanding, he must move from the position of being in equilibrium with his environment, because only when disequilibrium occurs does the learner's structure grow sharp enough to see inconsistencies in the way he understands something.

Note that in the foregoing paragraph the statement is made that the *learner* must move from a state of equilibrium; one cannot move him. That, of course, means that just telling the learner that his views of something are skewed does no good; he himself must make that discovery. He must be confronted with contradictory or new evidence that will disturb his equilibrium. That new and/or contradictory evidence must be *his own*, and the only way he gains that evidence is through inquiry. Through successive disequilibrations the child's cognitive structures are changed. This constant change of structure leads to intellectual development and explains why a stimulus seems to be delivered to a response. As Piaget says in the quotation earlier in this chapter, the response was present in the organism's structure before the stimulus, and the stimulus did not *generate* the response. But that response would not have been there if structures had not been built up through experiences that caused equilibration and disequilibration time and time again. Thus the stimulus-response view of learning is incomplete and inadequate without the concepts of equilibration and cognitive structures. Equilibration is, according to

Building mental structures about geometrical shapes requires experience with objects.

Phillips, an "overarching principle."[6] It is the one concept that ties together all the pieces of the cognitive view of learning.

Factors Affecting the Changing of Cognitive Structure

The discussion so far has assumed that intellectual development is dependent upon the changing of the learner's cognitive structures. We have also seen that those structures change through equilibration and disequilibration; thus the equilibrium concept is one of the important factors in cognitive development. But equilibration is not independent of other factors, even though it is the fundamental idea in changing cognitive structures. The *maturation* process also influences the intellectual development of a child. The relationship between chronological age and the intellectual level of the child will be considered later in this chapter.

[6]*Ibid.*

To help you isolate the next factor which influences cognitive development, you are asked to do an experiment. What do you hear when you read this sentence? The government should outlaw automobiles because they are the major contributors to air pollution, which is probably injurious to our health. Write down your "hearings" on a sheet of paper.

Now the experiment. Read the statement to three other persons and write down their "hearings."

We have done such an experiment, and we found that the persons we asked heard different things. Some of them fastened their attention on government; others argued that automobiles which were electric were not contributors; some said that many factors in our environment were injurious to our health; and still others insisted that there are many objects and functions in our society that are doing more damage to our air than automobiles are. In other words, the same words called to mind different focuses of attention for different people. Word meaning is not in the word itself; it is in the person hearing it. (How did your results correlate with ours?) All of us attach meaning to anything from our personal-language frame of reference. We are truly trapped in our language, and that is a tremendously important notion when we begin to think about changing a person's cognitive structure.

Earlier we saw that structures are changed by disturbing the learner's equilibrium. That equilibrium can be disturbed by communication with him, but when his language development is severely retarded; he is difficult to communicate with and difficult to disequilibrate. Consequently, changing the cognitive structures of learners with language deficiencies is more difficult than changing those of learners who have no such deficiency. How is language developed? It is developed through social interaction with other human beings. Piaget has called this factor *social transmission*. A learner cannot be disequilibrated if he is not in a position to receive information, and if his language development is not sufficient to perceive what is being said, he cannot receive the information. You have probably heard the phrase that every teacher should be a teacher of language. Most teachers interpret that phrase as meaning that they should teach grammar, and a few of them have done so. If teachers would interpret the universal direction to teach language to mean that they are responsible for leading a child to describe and receive information about his environment, they would be doing much more than teaching language; they would be moving the learner into a position where he could have his cognitive thinking changed through the disequilibration-equilibration process. By teaching a learner language he can use in describing his environment, we mean, of course, that this language development will occur as a result of *experiences* the learner has had.

That factor—experience—is the fourth factor that Piaget states has an influence upon cognitive-structure development. There are, according to Piaget, two kinds of experience—*physical* and *logico-mathematical.* Physical experience occurs when a learner interacts with objects in his environment and the environment itself. This kind of experience is essential to the very young learner. Through such interaction he begins to develop structures about objects, environments, and their interactions. Physical experience is also needed by many adolescents because their intellectual development has not reached the point where experience involving logic has any meaning for them. In fact, any adult encountering a new and unusual notion will have or attempt to secure physical or interactive experience because basic cognitive structures must be built when one is learning about something new. Those fundamental structures are probably best constructed, where possible, through physical experience in which information is obtained from objects themselves.

At some point in a child's education he begins to learn such things as that when he counts four groups of three objects he gets the same total as he does from counting three groups of four objects. He has learned that performing some *action* (rearranging) on the objects does not change their total number

[7]Piaget, "Development and Learning," *Journal of Research in Science Teaching*, Vol. 2, No. 3 (1964), 180.

Experience interacting with the materials of the world encourages actions to be internalized and so become operations.

While he is still manipulating objects, he is learning from the actions and not from the objects themselves. Such experiences Piaget has called *logico-mathematical*; these are experiences in which knowledge comes from the operations and not from the objects. In the foregoing example, Piaget says that when the learner

learns that the sum is independent of counting he is discovering the properties of the actions of ordering and uniting. He is learning something from the actions themselves, rather than from the objects independent of these actions. [8]

You probably noted that in the last paragraph the term *action* was introduced and that the example given was a physical

[8]Jean Piaget, "Foreword," in Millie Almy, *Young Children's Thinking*, (New York, Teachers College Press, Columbia University, 1966), vi.

action, that is, rearranging the objects. We also have stated that the learner acquires knowledge from the action. Or, as Piaget has said, ". . . a child learns very little . . . when experiments [investigations] are performed for him, . . . he must do them himself rather than sit and watch them done."[9] Learning from logico-mathematical experiences takes place only when the actions are internalized, that is, they are taken into the learner's cognitive structure, and he is then able to make decisions on the basis of his internalized actions and not on the basis of the physical manipulations. Such internalized actions are called *operations* and are the foundations of logico-mathematical experience. These experiences require that the learner coordinate his actions very carefully in order to avoid contradictions. He must, in other words, utilize a good deal of self-regulation, or contradictions will continually dominate his reasoning patterns. Self-regulation is the learner's own mechanism for utilizing the equilibrium concept. As he exercises his self-regulation, he checks his logic and seeks out contradictions that might be there. Finding those contradictions enables him to sharpen his structures and thus throw himself out of equilibrium and put himself back in. This, however, will occur only when the learner can internalize his actions and reverse his reasoning to get back to the beginning from any point in his line of reasoning. Children in the early years of school cannot reverse their thinking, and that explains why they cannot have logico-mathematical experiences.

By this time you are probably asking yourself, "What do these four factors have to do with classroom teaching?" If you have not, ask yourself right now, provide yourself an answer and write it down. Do not read on until you have formulated and recorded your answer. Remember, you are your own evaluator.

So far the learner has been referred to as having equilibrium destroyed and reestablished by interacting with objects and the

[9]*Ibid.*, v.

environment. The emphasis has been on the *learner's* inter-acting. This means that the teacher must ascertain the student's levels of language and intellectual development and then provide experience commensurate with his language and intellectual maturity level, which will permit him eventually to reach the point where he can change his own structures by learning from operations instead of having to rely continually on the information he gains directly from objects. While the learner is developing operational ability, he must be allowed a *maximum of activity* to investigate and interact with the materials of the discipline being studied. This general teaching direction applies not only to the way children get information from objects—physical experience—but also to logico-mathematical experience. Piaget sums up his beliefs about this latter kind of experience:

In the area of logico-mathematical structures, children have real understanding only of that which they invent themselves, and each time that we try to teach them something too quickly, we keep them from reinventing it themselves.[10]

In other words, Piaget's theories about how experience aids the intellectual development of the learner demand that teachers utilize exploration, invention, and discovery,[11] that is, inquiry, in all classrooms, for all subject matter, and at all grade levels.

Levels of Development

At several places in this chapter the point has been made that content must be selected which does not exceed a child's level of development and that most logico-mathematical experiences are beyond the level of children in the early grades. We hope

[10]*Ibid.*, vi.

[11]For a succinct discussion of the concepts of exploration, invention, and discovery see John W. Renner, Don G. Stafford, and William B. Ragan, *Teaching Science in the Elementary School* (2d ed., New York, Harper and Row, 1973), Chap. 7.

that you have been asking what the characteristics of learners at various intellectual levels are and how you can determine those levels. If you have not, skim back through the chapter and find those sections that discuss the intellectual level of the learner, and perhaps that will give you a frame of reference for what follows. One additional point—the intellectual-level concept for all children from kindergarten through grade thirteen is discussed in this book. Do not try to read only the part that is applicable to the particular level at which you teach. The intellectual-levels concept is a continuum, and to understand any part of it, the entirety must be viewed. Picking out only a portion of the continuum would be like attending a symphony concert and having hooked to your brain a sound filter that would allow you to hear only one instrument—you would never understand or appreciate the relationships among all the parts of the continuum.

Physical development of the human organism begins at conception, and cognitive development probably begins sometime before birth, though there is no evidence to support the latter statement. There are data available that trace the intellectual growth of children from birth, and the most nearly complete picture of that growth has been supplied by Piaget. His data tell him that the human animal has the ability to pass through *four* distinct intellectual-development phases from birth to death. When an individual is in each of these stages, his "mental functioning" has certain characteristics, or properties, and as he *begins to leave* one stage and *enter* another, those properties begin to change. Eventually his intellectual functioning undergoes a gradual but complete change and what was earlier impossible for him to do (that is, think about) he can now accomplish.

The picture of intellectual development that Piaget has constructed comes from data that he received in working directly with individual children over a period of many years. His methods of data collection are unique and are largely clinical; Phillips describes Piaget's method of operation.

He observes the child's surroundings and his behavior, formulates a hypothesis concerning the structure that underlies and includes them both, and then tests that hypothesis by altering the surroundings slightly—by rearranging the materials, by posing the problem in a different way, or even by overtly suggesting to the subject a response different from the one predicted by the theory.[12]

Perhaps for our purposes, Piaget's procedure for gathering data could be described as giving the child a task to perform that involves materials and reasoning, letting him perform the task, and then asking him what he did and why he did it that way. What is important for you as a teacher is that Piaget's model of intellectual development comes from *direct* association with learners of all ages. As a teacher you are directly associated with learners, and you should know that any model you use to guide you in selecting and employing content and materials must be relevant to children.

The First Level

The first stage of intellectual development in Piaget's model begins at birth and continues until the child is approximately two and one-half years old; he has called this period the *sensory-motor* phase. During this phase the child learns that objects are permanent, that just because an object disappears from sight does not mean that it no longer exists. During the sensory-motor period, language begins to develop, and that development is far too complex to explore fully in this book.[13] Basically, however, the child learns to attach sounds to the objects, symbols, and experiences he has had. But this inventing of appropriate sounds for something depends, as does later learning, on the child's having an experience with that something. It is during the sensory-motor period that the first signs begin to emerge that intellect is developed and does not just occur. Now,

[12]Phillips, *The Origins of Intellect*, 4.
[13]*Ibid.*, 13–49. Phillips presents a thorough picture of the sensory-motor child.

certainly, the way a sensory-motor child goes about learning is quite different from the way it occurs in an adult, but throughout all the stages of Piaget's model the fact becomes obvious that later learning cannot occur "unless 'early learning' has been accomplished."[14] This means, for example, that for culturally deprived children who have not had the benefit of a rich environment to assist them in developing the beginnings of a language system the school may need to provide many experiences that go far beyond the conventional reading-readiness programs *before* traditional "school" activities can begin. There is little likelihood that many sensory-motor children will be found in the schools. You need to be aware, however, that this is the stage in which intellectual development begins to emerge and that, unless certain goals are accomplished *by the child* in this stage, later learning must wait. Perhaps we as teachers need to spend more time determining when the learner is ready to begin and less time being concerned about the specific content being covered.

The Second Level

Before the the second, or preoperational, stage of intellectual development in Piaget's model is investigated, two factors need to be thoroughly understood: the age at which each stage is entered and the passage from stage to stage within the model. There is only one stage in Piaget's model whose starting point can be precisely stated—the sensory-motor stage.Piaget has repeatedly pointed out the inexactness of the various ages at which certain types of intelligence begin to emerge. He has described that inexactness in this way: "To divide developmental continuity into stages recognizable by some set of external criteria is not the most profitable of occupations."[15] A two-and-one-half-year-old child will begin to enter the preoperational

---

[14]*Ibid.*, 17.

[15]Jean Piaget, *Psychology of Intelligence*, (Paterson, N.J., Littlefield, Adams & Co., 1963), 139.

stage, and his exodus from that kind of thinking begins *around seven years of age*. In other words, exact, precise ages at which a learner will progress from stage to stage in the model cannot be stated. As you have probably surmised, the child himself determines his progress through the stages. Piaget has described the relationship of the stages within his model and age: ". . . although the order of succession is constant, the chronological ages of these stages vary a great deal."[16] As you read the remainder of this discussion about Piaget's model of intellectual development, the misconception that a child moves *completely* from one stage to another can easily be developed. The evidence available suggests that a learner can easily be in the sensory-motor phase on some traits and preoperational on others. Rather than thinking about a child's moving *from* one stage *into* another, consider that he moves into a particular stage on certain traits. As his development progresses, he moves deeper and deeper into a particular stage on some traits, and he enters into the stage on other traits. In other words, there is not a chronological line, and as he passes it he has moved from one stage to another, much as he is permitted to vote when he reaches voting age. Within this paragraph the notion of "trait" has been referred to. What is a trait? Basing your comments *only* on what you know so far, describe your idea of the traits that have been referred to. To lead you to an understanding of Piaget's use of the concept of trait, we will utilize the preoperational stage of intellectual development.

Earlier in this chapter the concepts of *action* and *operation* were discussed. An action is something a child does that is mainly physical, and when an action is taken into the child's cognitive structure and he is able to reverse his thinking anywhere in the action and go back to the starting point, he has performed an operation. An operation is an intellectual procedure; an action may not be. Consider this example, which may

---

[16]Piaget, "Development and Learning," *Journal of Research in Science Teaching*, Vol. 2, No. 3 (1964), 178.

call up some bad memories for you. Perhaps at some time in your educational experience you were exposed to a mathematical formula that you did not completely understand—say, one like

$$S = \tfrac{1}{2}at^2, \quad x = \frac{-b \pm \sqrt{b^2 - 4ac}}{2a}, \text{ or } a = \frac{dv}{dt}.$$

Now suppose that, to take part in the great school trivia contests known as examinations, you had to use such a formula. We are willing to wager that you memorized the formula and several examples and then when necessary searched the problem presented to you for clues that let you apply a formula. In other words, you acted upon the problem with a number of formulas until you found a match. While there is a slight hint of operation in matching formula and problem, what was just described is primarily an action. Operations must be completely reversible and internalized by the learner. The name of the second stage of intellectual development in the Piagetian model, that is, preoperational, is wonderfully descriptive of what children at this age are like. They cannot mentally operate with ideas that require them to take information into their cognitive structures and do simple mental experiments with it. Perhaps the best description of the preoperational child is that he is *perception-bound*[17]—he sees, he decides, and he reports. In short, he thinks, but he cannot think about his own thinking.

A complete description of all the intellectual characteristics of the preoperational child is far beyond the scope of this book. If, after studying what is here, you wish to investigate further the characteristics of preoperational children, you are urged to consult the book written by John L. Phillips, Jr., which has been referred to throughout this chapter, or *The Psychology of*

---

[17]The authors wish that we could take credit for inventing this phrase, but we cannot. We first heard it used by Celia Stendler Lavatelli in the film *The Developmental Theory of Piaget: Conservation* (produced by John Davidson Films, San Francisco, 1969).

Intelligence, in which Piaget explains his intellectual model and the characteristics of the stages within the model. For the purposes of utilizing the Piagetian model in selecting and using content and instructional methodology, there are five basic characteristics of the preoperational child that warrant examination.[18] Those characteristics are (1) egocentrism, (2) irreversibility, (3) centering, (4) states and transformation, and (5) transductive reasoning.

Egocentrism in the young child is one of his most prominent preoperational traits; the child sees the world from only one point of view—his own. The world as far as he is concerned revolves around him, and he is unaware that he is a prisoner of a single frame of reference for viewing the world. In other words, the child cannot see another's point of view or take that point of view and coordinate it with his own and those of others. He has his own opinion, which his perception has given him, and he feels no responsibility to justify his reasoning nor look for contradictions in it. A preoperational learner has developed a certain language pattern with which he communicates, and he does not have the ability to adapt his language to the needs of his listeners. Considering his single frame of reference for viewing the world, the language patterns of a preoperational learner are entirely predictable. The learner in this stage of development loses his perception-bound view of the world and his environment by interacting with it, and that kind of experience must always be provided. He cannot gain any understanding of anything by being told about it or given its abstractions; he thinks only about what he perceives from his observations of and interaction with his surroundings. The egocentric trait of a child continues throughout the preoperational stage, which ends between six and one-half and seven and one-half years of age. Teachers of this age group must be continually aware that they have to provide experiences that

[18]The equilibration concept should be recalled while studying the stages in the Piagetian model; it was earlier called the "overarching concept of intellectual development."

permit the child to have a maximum of physical experience and a minimum (if any) of logico-mathematical experience. That fact raises serious questions about the viability of some of the firmly entrenched activities that are found in the early years of schooling. Reading, for example, begins basically as a set of abstract sounds that are represented by a series of abstract symbols. After all, why is a series of lines hooked in a certain way called "A", "B", or "C"? That series is defined, and we believe that it is an abstraction, and, in order to use it, the child must take another's point of view. That requirement contradicts the preoperational learner's egocentric trait. Is there a possibility that reading difficulties, which can plague a person his entire life, are begun when an egocentric, preoperational learner is placed in a situation where those in charge demand that he begin to internalize abstractions that he cannot comprehend? Comprehension of an abstraction demands that the learner take it into his cognitive structure and operate with it. According to the empirical data upon which the Piagetian model is based, a preoperational learner is not able to perform intellectual operations. Perhaps much of the time spent in teaching reading in the first grade could better be spent giving the children physical experiences with objects (some of which might be with letters) and social interactions that will lead them to develop a language structure much expanded from the one they bring to school. (Reading and the preoperational child will be examined in chapter 3.)

Reading, however, is not the only subject area that needs to be critically examined from the preoperational child's egocentric point of view. It must be remembered that the egocentric child is perception-bound. That means that his understandings of the social world must be developed from experience. In early elementary grades a social-studies program that concentrates upon such topics as "Children of Other Lands," for example, is of questionable value. Perception of the children of other lands is not possible.

The second trait of the preoperational child that has great

importance from the curriculum-methodology frame of reference is that of *irreversibility*. For a human organism to begin to do intellectual operations, he must be able to reverse his thinking. The irreversibility of thought is beautifully illustrated by this dialogue with an eight-year-old boy:

> Have you got a brother?
> Yes.
> And your brother, has he got a brother?
> No.
> Are you sure?
> Yes.
> And has your sister got a brother?
> No.
> You have a sister?
> Yes.
> And she has a brother.
> Yes.
> How many?
> No, she hasn't got any.
> Is your brother also your sister's brother?
> No.
> And has your brother got a sister?
> No.[19]

The dialogue with the child continues until he finally recognizes that he is his brother's brother. This dialogue with a four-year-old girl also nicely demonstrates the irreversibility concept:

> Have you got a sister?
> Yes.
> And has she got a sister?
> No, she hasn't got a sister. I am my sister.[20]

Reversibility means that a thought is capable of being returned to its starting point. For example: $8+6=14$, and $14-6=8$. The

---

[19]Jean Piaget, *Judgment and Reasoning in the Child*, (Paterson, N.J., Littlefield, Adams, & Co., 1964), 86.

[20]*Ibid.*, 85.

thought started with 8 and returned to 8. Preoperational children cannot reverse their thinking. Consider what that says to those planning a mathematics program for early primary grades. Is there a possibility that mathematics activities, which require mental reversibility in order to achieve understanding, are introduced into the early elementary grades, and, since the learners cannot mentally reverse, they memorize for the trivia contests? Could it be that such an experience creates problems with mathematics that individuals never conquer?

Isolating the irreversible trait in a young child's thinking is not difficult and is informative. The following procedure will allow you to do it. The materials you will need are simple—two equal quantities of modeling clay or Plasticene—we have found that using different-colored pieces facilitates communication with the child (a five-year-old child will probably be best to work with). Form the pieces of clay into two balls and explain to the child that you want to start the experiment with one ball just the same size as the other. Allow your subject to work with the two balls until he believes they are just the same size. Now deform one of the balls; a good way to do this is to roll one of the balls into a long, cylindrical shape. Next ask the child whether there is more clay in the ball, more in the roll, or whether there is the same amount in each (be sure to give him all three choices), and ask him why he believes as he does. Record the child's answer and his reasoning. A child who has not developed the thinking trait of reversibility will tell you that there are different amounts in the two clay shapes. Our experience has been that most preoperational children will select the cylinder shape as containing more clay.

The subject you tested (if he is preoperational) is not able to make the reversal in his thinking from the cylinder-shaped object back to the clay sphere. He cannot do the analyzing and synthesizing that would permit him mentally to reconstruct the sphere, although he knows that it existed. That can be proved by asking the child to restore the roll of clay to its original shape, and he will produce a sphere and now tell you

Games require the use of reversibility and move children deeper and deeper into the concrete stage of thought.

there is the same amount of clay in each. At this age the child thinks, but he is so irreversible that he cannot think about his thinking.

Why does the learner *usually* focus his attention on the cylinder-shaped object rather than on the ball? That is explained by another trait in the preoperational model—*centering*. When the clay ball is deformed, the child probably fixes his attention on the detail of length, and his rigid, perception-bound thinking structure prevents him from seeing anything else about the transformed object. In educational experiences provided for young children the teacher should avoid using materials and/or activities that encourage the centering trait. If, for example, colors are used, they should be attractive and appealing. Teachers must not be surprised when a child focuses his attention upon one aspect of an object, event, or situation; he is only acting as a preoperational learner can be expected to act. Insisting that a child decenter and consider other aspects of an object will not prove fruitful. The teacher can be so insistent that the child says he sees some other property just to get the teacher to leave him alone, and nothing is accomplished. Centering is a characteristic of preoperational children, and those working with them should expect to find it. Does a child's inability to reverse his thinking cause him to center, or does his centering trait cause irreversibility? Who knows? Besides, is it important? Both traits exist, and which comes first is really not relevant because obviously they are not mutually exclusive.

The extreme perception-boundness of a preoperational child is well illustrated by the trait known as *states and transformations*. Figure 1 represents a wooden rod that is standing vertically (position 1) and is then released (positions 2 to 5). The rod eventually comes to rest at position 6. The rod is in a state of rest when it is held in position 1 and is again in a state of rest in position 6. If a series of pictures were taken of the falling object, it would be seen to pass through many other states, as represented by positions 2 to 5. In other words, the series of states in the event results in a *transformation* from the stick standing erect to its horizontal position.

If a preoperational child is shown the experiment, after having been informed that he will be asked to draw a diagram of it, he will not draw what is shown in Figure 1, nor will he indicate in any way what successive states the stick goes through in being transformed from position 1 to position 6. Our experience in asking children to do this task has been that they draw only positions 1 and 6. They see only the beginning and final states and do not see the transformation. This particular preoperational trait (which also shows irreversibility and centering) is particularly important when young children are being taught a process, for example, a plant-growing experiment. There is little need to try to get them to see the importance of the several states in the transformation; they cannot do it. They will perceive the first and final states and nothing else. The process that allows the final state to be a function of the intermediate states cannot be seen by preopera-

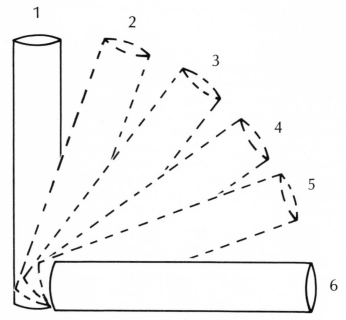

Fig 1. Transformation

tional children. That trait seems to call into doubt the system of providing young children music lessons in which a technique is to be learned (there are classic exceptions, such as Mozart), mathematical processes such as subtraction, and the techniques of spelling.

In Piaget's book *Play, Dreams and Imitation in Childhood* he relates the following incident that occurred when his daughter Jacqueline was just past two years old:

[She] wanted a doll-dress that was up-stairs: She said *"Dress"*, and when her mother refused to get it, "Daddy get dress." As I also refused, she wanted to go herself, "To mummy's room." After several repetitions of this she was told that it was too cold there. There was a long silence, and then: "Not too cold.—Where?—In the room.—Why isn't it too cold?—Get dress."[21]

[21]Trans. by C. Gutlegno and F. M. Hodgson (New York, W. W. Norton & Co., Inc., 1951), 230–31. The original French edition was published in 1945.

As far as Jacqueline was concerned, there was no difference in the logic between the fact that a warm room makes securing the dress possible and that getting the dress makes the room warm. Jacqueline was reasoning from particular to particular and not from general to particular (deduction) or particular to general (induction). Piaget has called the particular-to-particular reasoning *transduction*. This kind of reasoning begins to appear in the child with the beginning of language and lasts until about four years of age. Here is an example of transductive thought:

Daphne wanted me to show her how to blow bubbles with bubble gum. She gave me a piece that was rather grainy and would not form large bubbles at all. After several attempts at blowing a bubble without success, I told her that the bubble gum was not good. She began giving me instructions on how to get the bubble to become big. She told me to take a deep breath, blow until the bubble gum and air got all mixed together, and then blow again.

I tried again to blow a bubble, following her instructions, but to no avail. She looked at the pens in my pocket and said, "It's probably the pencils that keep you from blowing the bubbles." I told her she could take them out if she wanted to, and she did. Again I tried to blow a bubble and it didn't work. Undaunted, she looked around for some other cause and decided that her bicycle (which was sitting in the living room near the chair in which we were sitting) was causing our problem. She moved the bicycle to the other side of the room, and then came back to see if I could blow a bubble.

After failing to get a bubble blown without its popping, I told her again that the gum was no good for blowing bubbles. This reason still did not satisfy her. She then decided that a bug was popping the bubbles (there were no bugs in sight). She ran to the kitchen, got the fly swatter, and came back to the living room to chase the imaginary bug. She hit a couple of things with the fly swatter and then came running back to see if I could blow a bubble. Of course, I couldn't.

By this time she had given up on the bubbles and me, so I rather happily spit out the bubble gum, which had lost all semblance of flavor.

That evening, I asked her if she ever decided why I couldn't blow bubbles for her. "I sure did", she replied. "It was those stupid flies and the bubble gum wasn't any good".[22]

As a teacher, do not be surprised if you encounter transduction in kindergarten and first-grade children. If you do, be patient; usually it disappears with the increased experiences a school environment can provide over what the preschool environment supplied.

Identifying the Preoperational Thinker

Identifying whether or not the preoperational thinker can see the relationships between states and transformations is a simple task; do the falling-stick experiment with the child and then ask him to tell you what happened. Identifying egocentrism, irreversibility, centering, and transduction, however, is not as easy as using the falling-stick experiment.

There is, however, a procedure that can be used to identify preoperational children, and you have already met one of the techniques used — the clay-balls activity used to illustrate irreversibility in thinking. That activity can be described as illustrating the *inability* of a preoperational child to hold mentally the image of an object and see that distorting the object does not change the amount of material it contains. "Mentally holding" the original image of an object is called *conservation reasoning*, and preoperational children do not conserve — that is, they make decisions about the distortion of the object on the basis of what they perceive. This rigid perception-boundness, however, is due to such traits as irreversible thinking, tendency to center, extreme egocentrism, inability to see a transformation among several states, and transductive reasoning. In other words, identifying a child who does not conserve will

[22]We are grateful to William Fix, who thoughtfully and completely recorded this example of transductive reasoning exhibited by his forty-four-month-old daughter.

allow you to describe his stage of intellectual development in terms of such traits as the five preoperational traits already described. Conservation, then, is an overt manifestation of whether or not a child is a preoperational thinker. Chapter 2 involves you with the conservation-reasoning abilities of the child and the impact of educational experiences on the acquisition of those abilities.

2. Development of Conservation Reasoning Through Experience

Donald G. Stafford and John W. Renner

The research of Piaget has led him to conclude that the ability to use conservation reasoning appears at about seven years of age. He has also developed several tasks that allow a child to demonstrate his ability to utilize conservation reasoning. In our work we utilized six conservation tasks: conservation of number, liquid amount, solid amount, weight, length, and area.

1. *Conservation of number.* A stack of red and a stack of black checkers were placed in front of the child. The child was then told that the tester was going to form a row of black checkers, and that each time the tester placed a checker into the row the child was to place a red checker alongside it so that the two rows would contain the same number of checkers. Seven checkers of each color were used to make each row (Figure 2,

Data indicate that the conservation of number is one of the early reasoning abilities acquired.

Arrangement A

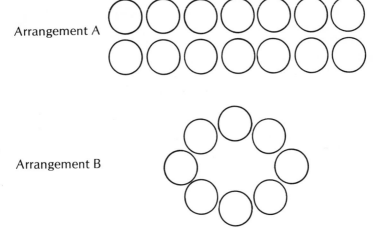

Arrangement B

Fig. 2. Conservation of number

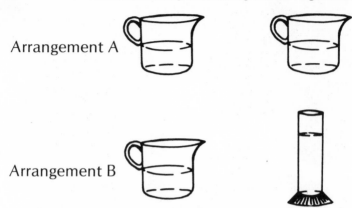

Fig. 3. Conservation of liquid amount

Arrangement A) so that the child could count them if he wanted to do so. After completion of the row the tester asked the child whether each of the two rows contained exactly the same number of checkers. When the child agreed that each row did contain the same number of checkers, the tester then rearranged the black checkers to form a circle (Figure 2, Arrangement B) and again asked whether the numbers of black and red checkers were the same. If the child indicated that the numbers of checkers were still the same, that was taken as adequate evidence that he conserved number.

2. *Conservation of liquid amount.* Three glasses, two wide measuring glasses of equal size, marked in one-eighth cup gradations and one tall, narrow, unmarked cylinder, were used in this test. The two wide glasses were filled to the one-cup mark with red-colored water. The child was then told, "Let's pretend we are having a party, and this is your Kool-Aid, and this glass is mine. Do we have the same amount to drink?" If the child said that one glass contained more or was not certain, he was asked to add or take away liquid until he felt certain that they were the same (Figure 3, Arrangement A). At this point the tester poured his glass of Kool-Aid into the tall, narrow

Those mental structures that allow a child to conserve liquid amount are not normally acquired until about the age of six years. Photo by Don Cook, courtesy *Ada Evening News*.

cylinder (Figure 3, Arrangement B). He then repeated the question, "Do we each have the same amount to drink now?" An affirmative answer was taken as evidence that the child conserved liquid amount.

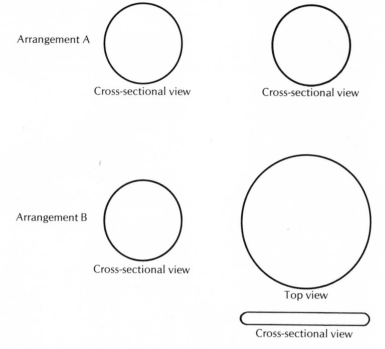

Fig. 4. Conservation of solid amount

3. *Conservation of solid amount.* Two balls of red Plasticene were placed in front of the child. The child was then told to imagine that this was something very good to eat and was told, "This is your piece to eat, and this one is mine. Do we each have the same amount to eat?" If the child agreed that each ball contained the same amount, the test continued. If he did not believe that the two amounts were the same, he was asked to take from one ball and add to the other until they contained the same amount (Figure 4, Arrangement A). When the child had decided that each ball contained the same amount to eat, the tester took one ball and, in full view of the child, flattened it into a pancake shape and again placed it alongside the ball (Figure 4, Arrangement B). Pointing to the pancake-shaped piece of Plasticene, the tester said, "This is my piece to eat and

that is yours. Do we have the same amount to eat?" An affirmative answer was considered to be adequate evidence that the child conserved solid amount.

4. *Conservation of weight.* Two balls of blue Plasticene approximately the same size were placed in front of the child (Figure 5, Arrangement A). One ball was then handed to the child with the question, "Is it heavy?" When the child's attention was considered to be focused on the heaviness of the ball, the second ball of Plasticene was handed to the child with this question ⌐ ⌐ter, "Is this ball just as heavy as the other one. ⌐vier than the other?" If the child said th⌐ he was asked to take from one ball ⌐. After the child had decided t⌐ tester took one ball and in ⌐asticene into a bowl (Figure ⌐en placed the bowl, open side

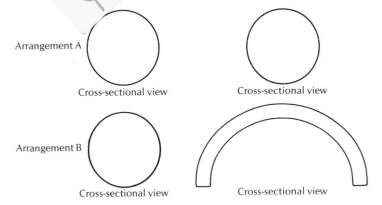

Arrangement A

Cross-sectional view   Cross-sectional view

Arrangement B

Cross-sectional view   Cross-sectional view

Fig. 5. Conservation of weight

down, in front of the child and beside the ball. He then asked, indicating each object in turn by placing his finger on it, "Is this one just as heavy as this one, or is one of them heavier?" The child was allowed to pick up the pieces of Plasticene if he wanted to for comparison (almost all the children did). If the child's reply indicated that he believed the two objects still weighed the same, this was taken as evidence that he conserved weight.

5. *Conservation of length*. The materials for this test consisted of two identical strings of beads, a small plastic horse, and two cubes of wood. The two strings of beads were laid side by side on the table in front of the child so that the ends matched. The child's attention was called to the fact that it was just as far from the end of one string of beads as it was from the other. The tester then said to the child, "Let's pretend that each string of beads is a road. I am going to place hay at the other end. If the horse walks down either of the roads, it would be just as far to the hay" (Figure 6, Arrangement A). When the child agreed that the distance was the same, the tester then bent one string of beads (as shown in Figure 6, Arrangement B) and asked, "Now, if the horse must follow the road, would

Arrangement A

Arrangement B

Fig. 6. Conservation of length

The mental structures that permit conserving length are not often found in young children. Photo by Don Cook, courtesy *Ada Evening News*.

he have to walk as far to the hay on one road as on the other?" If the child stated that the horse had to travel the same distance in either case, this was taken as evidence of conservation of length.

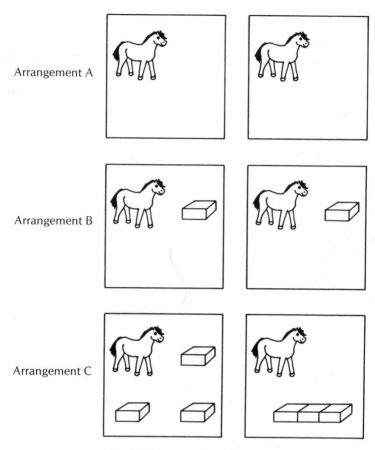

Fig. 7. Conservation of area

6. *Conservation of area.* The materials for this test were two sheets of one-foot-square green poster board, two plastic horses, and six red cubes three-fourths inch on each edge. The two sheets were placed in front of the child, one stacked on the other to show that they were equal in size. The sheets were then separated and placed in front of the child. The tester told the child, "Let's pretend that each of these is a patch of grass, and there is just as much grass on one patch as the other." A small plastic horse was placed in the same position on each board with the comment, "Each horse may eat all of the grass in his

Rearranging the "barns" is often necessary when considering the conservation-of-area task. Courtesy *Norman Transcript.*

patch if he wants to, and one has just as much to eat as the other (Figure 7, Arrangement A). Now I'm going to build a barn on each patch of grass and cover up some of it so that the horse can't get to it (Figure 7, Arrangement B). Is there just as much grass left for one horse to eat as the other?" If a negative answer was given and maintained after the test was repeated to this point, the child was listed as a nonconserver. Those children who answered affirmatively were then told, "I am going to build two more barns on each patch of grass, but I am going to build them beside the first barn on one patch of grass, and spread them out on the other patch (Figure 7, Arrangement C). Does each horse still have the same amount of grass to eat, or does one have more than the other?" An answer indicating that each horse still had the same amount of grass to eat was accepted as evidence that the child conserved area.

The foregoing tasks were administered to 252 children, one at a time. The children were randomly selected from the same school system. Each child was seated at a table on which clay,

43

checkers, and various other materials used in the tests were placed. The tester would say, "I would like you to help me by answering the questions I am going to ask you about these objects. You may touch any of the objects we are talking about if you want to, and I want you to tell me just what you think when I ask a question." Each child was given as much time as he wanted to think before replying to a question.

Table 1 shows the results of administering to each of the 252 children the six tasks of conservation described above.[1] The number shown in each cell of the table represents those who successfully completed that task. The heavy line running through Table 1 shows how conservers are divided from non-conservers by using Piaget's 75 per cent rule.[2] The line was drawn below the first cell containing nine positive responses and was followed by cells containing eight or more cases. If the cells following the *first* cell containing nine, contained less than eight, we assumed that the first cell containing nine was spurious. This is best illustrated by considering the "Area" column. A cell containing nine members if first encountered at 85 to 88 months, but not until 137 to 140 months, is a cell containing nine cases not followed by one containing less than eight.

The data in Table 1 clearly show that the conservation-of-area task is the most difficult. That task is followed in difficulty by length and then weight. Piaget has stated that the weight is not conserved until about ten years of age,[3] and our data support his conclusions. The conservation of solid amount is accomplished, according to Piaget "between seven and eight years of age." Again, our data corroborate his findings. Piaget

[1]John W. Renner, Judith Brock, Sue Heath, Mildren Laughlin, and Jo Stevens, "Piaget Is Practical," *Science and Children*, Vol. 9, No. 2 (October, 1971), 23.
[2]"We have followed the accepted custom of considering a test successfully passed when at least 75 per cent of the children of the same age have answered correctly." Piaget, *Judgment and Reasoning in the Child*, 100.
[3]Piaget, *Psychology of Intelligence*, 147.

Age in months	Sample Size	Number	Solid Amount	Liquid Amount	Length	Area	Weight
60– 64	12	3	2	2	2	1	1
65– 68	12	7	2		2	2	2
69– 72	12	6	3	4	1	1	1
73– 76	12	8	7	7	3	6	2
77– 80	12	8	5	3	3	2	6
81– 84	12	9	5	3		1	1
85– 88	12	11	11	9	6	9	10
89– 92	12	11	9	11	9	8	11
93– 96	12	9	9	8	7	6	8
97–100	12	12	12	11	9	8	11
101–104	12	12	11	8	5	7	8
105–108	12	11	9	9	7	8	10
109–112	12	11	10	10	7	7	6
113–116	12	11	11	10	7	7	7
117–120	12	12	12	10	7	6	9
121–124	12	9	12	11	7	8	9
125–128	12	11	11	10	9	7	11
129–132	12	12	11	11	12	10	10
133–136	12	12	12	12	8	7	12
137–140	12	12	10	10	10	10	12
141–146	12	12	12	12	12	12	12

Table 1. Conservation

has also stated that length and area are conserved between seven and eight years of age.[4] The children in our sample achieved those conservations somewhat later.

The data in Table 1 clearly show that the attainment of conservation reasoning is a gradual process. A child does not reach the concrete operational stage all at once. He enters into it, and, as he grows older and gains in experience, he moves more and more deeply into that stage.

Conservation and Curriculum

Now that evidence of the level of conservation reasoning in children has been determined, the next questions asked by the investigators are: Can the attainment of the conservation reasoning be significantly accelerated by experiences, expecially classroom experiences? If so, what kinds of experiences are needed?

Although efforts by investigators attempting to teach conservation directly have met with very limited success and frequently total failure, Joachim F. Wohlwill, of Clark University, who for several years has been involved in research in the area of intellectual development offers this opinion:

Our finding that children's scores (on conservation related tasks) could be raised by intensive experience suggests a profitable focus for instruction in the primary grades when little attention is usually given to cultivating the child's measuring and classifying skills. Our guess is that concerted efforts to encourage and guide children's activities in this area might pay handsome dividends.[5]

Millie Almy, who has also made extensive studies of child development, concurs with Wohlwill:

. . . it is interesting to note that most studies reported in the literature to date have worked with what seem to be the elements imme-

---

[4]*Ibid.*, 145.

[5]Joachim F. Wohlwill, "The Case of the Prelogical Child," *Psychology Today*, July, 1967, p. 25.

diately involved in the conservation task, such as addition and subtraction or reversibility, rather than with what may well be the developmentally prior abilities of classifying and ordering. . . . Piaget's work would suggest that children who have had many opportunities to classify objects on the basis of similar properties, to order along dimensions of difference, or better opportunities of both kinds, might arrive at a level of operational thought represented in conservation sooner than children who have not had such opportunities.[6]

The suggestions by Almy and Wohlwill set the stage for our investigation to determine whether the first-grade program of the Science Curriculum Improvement Study (SCIS) would accelerate the ability to conserve. This program was chosen because it was considered one of those most likely to accelerate the attainment of the conservations. First, instead of a short-range training program, the first-year program of SCIS is designed to extend over most of the school year, and second, according to the authors, the program "confronts the elementary school children with first-hand experiences of natural phenomena and with intellectual challenges that will stimulate their further cognitive development."[7] The experiences of the program are describing, grouping on the basis of property, serial ordering, and making generalizations and predictions. Emphasis is placed on direct experiences with real objects rather than on pictures or words.

The *SCIS Elementary Science Sourcebook*, designed to help teachers implement the program, states the following as a goal of the SCIS program: "The SCIS program aims to nurture the ability to discover new relationships and to think imaginatively, at the same time as it facilitates the transition from pre-operational to operational thought."[8]

[6]Almy, *Young Children's Thinking*, 125–26.
[7]Robert Karplus, *One Physicist Looks at Science Education*, (Berkeley, Science Curriculum Improvement Study, University of California, 1963), 6.
[8]Willard Jacobson and Allan Kondo, *SCIS Elementary Science Sourcebook* (Berkeley, University of California, 1968), 31.

The design of the research to determine whether the experience of the SCIS first-year program did accelerate the attainment of conservation reasoning was simple. An experimental group that used the SCIS program and a control group that used a traditional science program were selected. A pretest and a posttest of conservation tasks were administered to each group, and the gain in conservation reasoning was compared.

For our research experimental and control samples, each consisting of sixty first-grade children, were selected from elementary schools of the Norman, Oklahoma, school system. The schools that were selected offered essentially the same first-grade program *except* for science. The experimental sample was taken from three schools using the SCIS first-grade curriculum; the control group was taken from two schools providing a traditional science program. Table 2 provides a comparison of the experimental and control samples.

Information tabulated in Table 2 suggests that, although the schools were as carefully matched as possible in the opinions of officials from within the school system, the control had a slight advantage in almost every area of comparison. The average scores on both IQ and readiness test favored the control group. The number of children with above-average IQ was higher, and the number of children in the superior readiness score range for the control group was almost twice that of the experimental group; the number of children in the low normal range for the experimental group was almost two and one-half times that of the control group.

The pretest was given to experimental and control groups in September, during the second week of the fall school term. This test consisted of the conservation tasks in number, liquid amount, solid amount, weight, length, and area described earlier in this chapter. Posttests, which were identical to the pretests, were administered in January, at the end of the first semester of school. During the testing the children were not prompted on the correctness of their responses, since such prompting might enhance the training effects of the test. Also, only two categories of responses were recorded for each conservation test—conserver or nonconserver. Table 3 displays the results of the pretesting and posttesting. The number in each column represents the number of children out of sixty conserving on each task.

Table 2. Comparison of Experimental and Control Groups on the Data Provided by the Teacher

Data	Experimental Group	Control Group
Average IQ (Otis-Lennon)	103.2	106.2
Number of children in sample with IQ above 111 (above-average group)	17	21
Number of children in sample with IQ between 88 and 111 (average group)	33	34
Number of children in sample with IQ below 88 (below-average group)	10	5
Number of children who attended kindergarten	42	48
Number of children in sample with readiness scores above 76 (superior)	12	21
Number of children in sample with readiness scores between 64 and 76 (high-normal)	12	14
Number of children in sample with readiness scores between 45 and 63 (average)	23	19
Number of children in sample with readiness scores between 24 and 44 (low-normal)	12	5
Number of children in sample with readiness scores below 24 (low)	1	1
Average score on readiness test	59.23	65.60
Number of children with older brothers or sisters at home	37	65.60
Average chronological age in months at time of first test	76.93	77

Table 3. Pretest and Posttest Totals for Experimental and Control Groups

Conservation area	Experimental Group		Control Group	
	Pretest	Posttest	Pretest	Posttest
Number	13	50	15	37
Weight	3	13	1	8
Liquid amount	5	25	5	19
Solid amount	5	26	5	22
Length	3	30	0	11
Area	6	31	13	34
Total	—	—	—	—
Conservations	35	175	39	131
Gain in conservations		140		92

A visual comparison of pretest results shown in Table 3 reveals very little difference in the scores on each separate conservation task with the exception of area. On the pretest the control-group scores were slightly higher in two categories (area and number), the experimental group scores were slightly higher in two areas (weight and length), and the two groups scored equally on the remaining two areas.

The results of the posttest are shown in Figure 8. Note that the experimental group outscored the control group on every conservation task except area. Even on that task (which the data in Table 1 show to be the most difficult) the experimental group far outgained the control group. The total gain in conservation is the difference in the total conservations on the posttest (T_2) and pretest (T_1), or $\Sigma T_2 - \Sigma T_1$. The experimental group shows an advantage on this comparison of 140 to 92, approximately 3 to 2, or 52 per cent. Figures 8 and 9 show the gain in conservation by each group during the experiment.

The chi-square values in Table 4 were computed by using the numerical increase in conservation in each area for the experimental and control groups, and the number of children

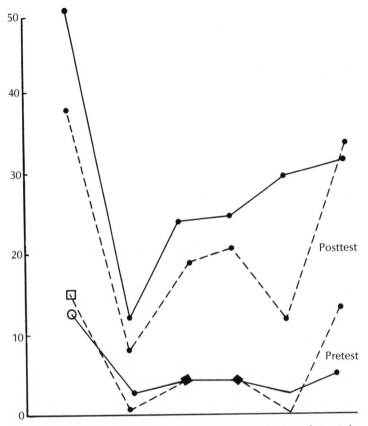

Fig. 8. Total conservations for each sample by task. Left to right: number, weight, liquid amount, solid amount, length, and area. The solid lines represent the experimental group; the dotted lines, the control group.

who were nonconservers in each were as determined by the pretest.

Two of the individual conservation areas (number and length) have chi-square values at the 1 per cent level of significance in favor of the experimental group. Also, the total numerical conservation increase based on the calculated possible

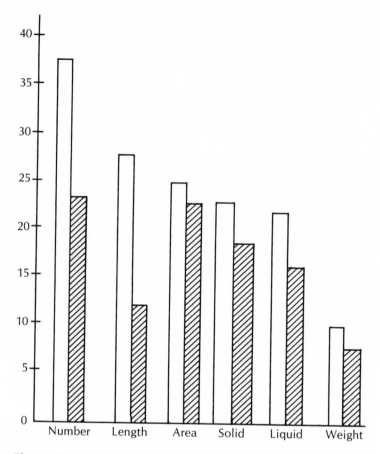

Fig. 9. Numerical gain in conservations. The open columns represent the experimental group; the shaded columns, the control group.

increase (360 minus the sum of conservations on the pretest) had a chi-square value with a significance at the 1 per cent level of confidence in favor of the experimental group. The conclusion was drawn that the experiences provided by the SCIS first-grade program significantly enhance the child's attainment of the ability to conserve, that is, to use conservation reasoning.

Data show that the first-grade program of the Science Curriculum Improvement Study builds mental structures that result in conservation reasoning. Courtesy Science Curriculum Improvement Study.

Table 4. Chi-Square Values and Levels of Significance for Numerical Increase in each Conservation Area

Hypothesis	Chi-Square Value	Significance Level
1. Number	8.90	0.01
2. Weight	0.75	0.40 (approximate)
3. Liquid amount	1.54	0.20 (approximate)
4. Solid amount	0.643	0.40 (approximate)
5. Length	11.25	0.01
6. Area	0.004	
7. Total conservations	14.25	0.01

Educational Implications

The suggestion was made early in this chapter that *the ability to use logic in problem solving is contingent on the acquisition of the thought processes which must be present before conservation reasoning is evident.* A child does not possess the ability to structure information for storage and efficient retrieval without the ability to use logic. Since achievement in all formal school activities presupposes the ability to store and retrieve information, it is imperative that every child be provided opportunities designed to develop and continuously refine this ability. The experiences made possible by the first-grade program of the SCIS have been shown to accelerate the attainment of conservation skills, which indicates the ability to use simple logic. This program of opportunities, initiated in the first grade or perhaps even in kindergarten, could make the entire educational program more meaningful and efficient.

Since the acceleration of the acquisition of conservation skills was achieved through educational experiences that were a part of normal curriculum, rather than a training exercise designed specifically to result in a particular conservation skill, it can be assumed that the acceleration was produced because the SCIS program provided a richer experiential educational environment than did the textbook program. The children apparently had prerequisite maturation and simply lacked the experiences needed to actuate the thought processes essential to conservation and logical thought. The experiences provided in the first-grade program of the SCIS are the kinds needed to initiate the movement toward the stated goal of the Educational Policies Commission: "the development of the ability to think."

We have shown that the first-grade program of SCIS does indeed enhance conservation reasoning. Are there specific beneficial results that can be pointed to as a result of this gain? The following quotation from Millie Almy describing her research findings led us to our next research effort.

. . . the findings in our studies of a rather substantial correlation between performance in conservation tasks and progress in beginning reading suggests that, to some extent, similar abilities are involved. A program designed to nurture logical thinking should contribute positively to reading readiness.[9]

Does the SCIS program, which nurtures logical thinking (conservation reasoning), actually have a positive influence on reading readiness? Experimental evidence presented in Chapter 3 answers this question.

[9]Almy, *Young Children's Thinking*, 139–40.

3. Experience, Conservation Reasoning, and Reading Readiness

Donald H. Kellogg

The research described in Chapter 2 demonstrated that providing children with experiences from the first-year program of the SCIS increased their ability to use conservation reasoning. In Chapter 1 the four factors that Piaget has said determined learning were listed—maturation, experience, social transmission, and equilibration. Working with the SCIS program certainly provides experiences for the children, and teaching the unit as its developers intended provides social transmission. Watching children work with the unit provides many opportunities to observe equilibration and disequilibration. Such evaluation is subjective, but hard data are available that demonstrate that experiences with the SCIS program lead children into the concrete operational stage. The evidence for that statement is found in the data of Chapter 2, showing that the first-year program of the SCIS increased the child's ability to use conservation reasoning.

The Hypothesis

The quotation from Millie Almy at the end of Chapter 2 served as the basic hypothesis for the research described in this chapter.

Since we had a vehicle (the first-year program of the SCIS) that nurtures logical thinking, it should also serve as a reading-readiness program that is superior to a readiness program not specifically designed to nurture such thinking. Our hypothesis was this: the SCIS first-year program is superior to the usual commercial program in producing readiness for reading in first-grade children.

Experimental

To test our hypothesis, we enlisted the aid of a school system different from that involved in the research described in Chapter 2. In preparation for this research a summer workshop gave the teachers an in-depth experience with teaching elementary school science by inquiry in general and the units developed by the SCIS in particular. During the following academic year those teaching the units were provided the assistance of a consultant to help in the implementation of the SCIS program. At the end of the academic year we believed that teachers who could teach the entire SCIS program, and in particular the "Material Objects" unit, were available to us.

Four first-grade classes were selected. The principal criterion for selection was that the teacher be thoroughly experienced in teaching the "Material Objects" unit. No attempt was made to move children from one class to another; we accepted them as they had enrolled. Owing to the enrollment patterns in the participating school system, there was no reason to believe that any one class had a different set of learner abilities from any other. The four classes were accepted as homogeneous and representative of the school population being studied. Two of the classes were randomly designated as the control group, and the other two became the experimental group.

The students in the control group experienced a commercial reading-readiness program, while at the same time the experimental group used the "Material Objects" unit and experienced no reading-readiness program. Both groups were given the *Metropolitan Reading Readiness Test*[1] at the beginning of the school year as a pretest and six weeks later were given a posttest, again using the *Metropolitan*.

The *Metropolitan* test provides scores on six subtests: word meaning, listening, matching, alphabet, numbers, copying, and a total score. The experimental group experienced "Material Objects" every day up to two hours at a time. This administration of the posttest coincided with the completion of the "Material Objects" unit by the experimental group.

The results of the pretesting and posttesting for both the experimental and control groups are shown in Table 5. In that table the mean gain on each subtest in the test for each group is given. You will immediately note that the experimental group *numerically outgained* the control group on all the subtests except copying. The gains in word meaning, matching, numbers, and total scores were substantially significant.

Table 5. Gains in Subtest Scores and Levels of Significance of That Change

Subtest	Control	Experimental	t value	Level of Significance
Word Meaning	0.43	1.62	1.9041	0.1 −>0.05
Listening	1.34	1.43	0.1377	Not significant
Matching	1.71	2.81	1.5426	0.2 −>0.1
Alphabet	3.84	4.29	0.5010	Not significant
Numbers	3.71	4.94	1.4599	0.2 −>0.1
Copying	1.43	1.29	−0.2202	Not significant
Total	12.81	16.35	1.4511	0.2 −>0.1

(N for control=32; N for experiment=37; degrees of freedom=67)

[1]*Metropolitan Reading Readiness Test* (New York, Harcourt, Brace and World, 1962).

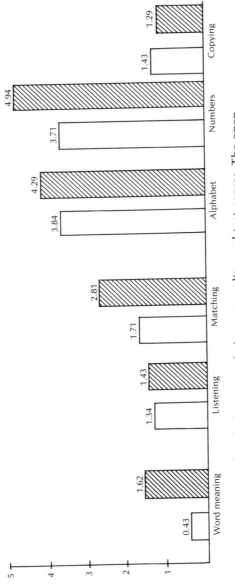

Fig. 10. Average gain in metropolitan subtest scores. The open columns represent the control group; the shaded columns, the experimental group.

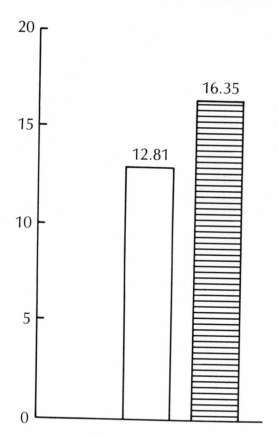

Fig. 11. Average gain in total metropolitan score. The open column represents the control group; the shaded column, the experimental group.

Figure 10 shows the gains on each subtest for the experimental and control groups. Figure 11 compares the total average gain made by the control and experimental groups on the entire test.

Data Interpretations

In light of the greater gains by the experimental group in five of the six subtest areas one is almost compelled to ask himself:

The experimental data led the authors to conclude that the "Material Objects" unit of the Science Curriculum Improvement Study is a superior reading-readiness program.

how can a science program outperform a reading-readiness program when compared on reading-readiness standards? The answer to this question lies in the examination of two factors: (1) the nature of the "Material Objects" unit and (2) the purpose of education.

We believe that the experimental group outperformed the control group in the areas of word meaning, listening, matching, and numbers because the members of the experimental group, through the use of the "Material Objects" units, were allowed to have concrete experiences in each of these areas to the limit of their interest and ability. The children learned to match because they were allowed to match properties to objects, using objects that they could grasp, manipulate, and even alter. They developed skills in listening because they listened to the teacher and to their fellow students describing, classifying, and

61

discussing experiences. They learned word meaning when words were invented by the teacher (or by themselves) as needed to describe experiences with objects. A number of skills were gained as they serial ordered objects or groups of objects. They were outgained on the copying subtest because they did not do much copying, but instead were allowed and encouraged to think. There does not seem to be an adequate explanation at this time for the superior gains of the experimental group on the alphabet subtest.

The second factor concerns a basic area, the purpose of education. In a 1961 statement the Educational Policies Commission said, "The purpose which runs through and strengthens all other educational purposes—the common thread of education—is the development of the ability to think."[2]

If this statement is accepted, and we do accept it, the implication is undeniable: To learn to read, the child must first have developed some ability in the reasoning process. A person need not be able to read in order to reason, but must a person be able to reason in order to read? We believe that, indeed, the answer to that question is yes, and our research supports that answer. Almy found that progress in beginning reading is related to performance in conservation tasks.[3] The data in Chapter 2 demonstrate that the use of the "Material Objects" unit promotes the attainment of conservation reasoning. The research described in this chapter shows that the use of "Material Objects" can help develop reading readiness. The conclusion, then, is: to best teach reading, first teach thinking, as represented by conservation reasoning.

Chapters 2 and 3 have been devoted to research into the interface that exists between preoperational and concrete operational reasoning and the impact that elementary school science curricula make upon moving into the concrete stage. The last

[2]Educational Policies Commission, *The Central Purpose of American Education* (Washington, D.C., National Education Association of the United States, 1961), 12.

[3]Almy, *Young Children's Thinking.*

stage in the Piagetian model, formal operational thought, will be discussed in the next five chapters, as well as its identification and the effect of inquiry-centered science programs upon student entry into that final stage.

4. Formal Operational Thought and Its Identification

John W. Renner

The *preoperational* thinker often indulges in fantasy that often has no basis in fact. If the world does not suit him, he imagines it to be different until he has the kind of fanciful world he wants. The *concrete-operational* thinker is concerned with the actual data he extracts from objects, the organization of those data, and the mental experiments he can do with them. This learner does not formulate hypotheses outside his realm of direct experience; he accommodates his thinking to events in the real world. He can categorize, compare, seriate, and perform other various acts that will lead to the extraction of information from objects if he is given experience with concrete objects, events, and/or situations. In short, the concrete-operational child does not depart from reality as the preoperational thinker does, even though those departures have no lawful or logical basis.

Somewhere around eleven years of age, according to Piaget,[1]

[1]Piaget, *Psychology of Intelligence*, 148.

there begins to emerge from concrete-operational thought minds that can be described as "concerned with reality, but reality is only a subset within a much larger set of possibilities."[2] A person with such thought processes Piaget has called *formal operational* and has described as "an individual who thinks beyond the present and forms theories about everything, delighting especially in consideration of that which is not."[3] The formal-operational thinker no longer is restricted to thinking only about concrete objects, events, and/or situations. He can now stretch his thinking far beyond reality and into the possible.

Formal-operational thinkers have the ability to take imaginative "trips," but the bases for their trips are firmly rooted in the reality of the information they receive from the world around them. Phillips explains the formal operational thinker as being "capable of departures from reality," but adds that "those departures are lawful."[4] A preoperational thinker cannot think about what it is he thinks. A concrete-operational thinker can think about his thinking, as long as objects are present for him to manipulate, and a formal-operational thinker can think about the consequences and/or implications of his thinking. He can think in the abstract and does not need objects to manipulate; he can take data and treat the pattern those data have as only one possible arrangement they might form. As was said earlier, reality is only one possibility as far as the formal, abstract thinker is concerned. *The possible is as real to him as the here and now.* Another way that may be useful in helping you think about the formal level is to remember that the preoperational thinker cannot do mental operations while the concrete thinker can perform mental operations with the information he has received from concrete objects. The formal-operational thinker not only performs mental operations with reality but also can perform operations on the operations used in mental experimentation.

[2]Phillips, *The Origins of Intellect: Piaget's Theory*, 101.
[3]Piaget, *Psychology of Intelligence*.
[4]Phillips, *The Origins of Intellect*.

Formal thinking has two constructs that are useful in its identification. The first of these constructs results from the understanding that a formal thinker has of the importance in his experimentation of keeping all factors constant except one—the one being varied. He has, therefore, a frame of reference, which says that, all other things being equal, such and such a variable has (or does not have) an effect on the outcome of the experiment. The ability of a child to handle the "all-other-things-being-equal" construct can lead you to suspect that you are working with a formal-operational learner. The second construct that is useful in identifying formal thinking and those who use it is that of the proposition. In fact, formal-operational thinking is often called propositional logic. Propositional thinking can be most easily thought of as being of this form: "If (such and such is true), then it follows that (such and such is true), therefore, this (action) is dictated (or suggested)." The "if, then, therefore," construct demands that the person using it depart from reality and push himself into the formation of hypotheses. Such is the ability and prerogative of the formal-operational thinker.

Identifying Formal Thought

Piaget and Inhelder have broken concrete operational thought into two substages, IIa and IIb.[5] The differences between these stages are subtle and can best be described by the differences in performance on the following tasks. Those researchers have also broken down the formal operations stage into two substages, IIIA and IIIB, and have stated that substage IIIA occurs between eleven and fourteen to fifteen years of age and substage IIIB from fourteen to fifteen years on.[6] Throughout the past several years, we have used the following tasks in identifying formal operational thought:

[5]Bärbel Inhelder and Jean Piaget, *The Growth of Logical Thinking* (New York, Basic Books, Inc., 1958), 7.
[6]*Ibid.*

1. The conservation of solid amount. As described earlier, the student was allowed to work with two balls of clay until he was convinced that each ball contained the same amount. The examiner then distorted one of the balls. The student was asked whether the distorted clay or the clay ball contained more clay or whether each contained the same amount. *This task and the one following were administered to establish whether the student was concrete-operational.* If he successfully completed the task, he was rated II*A* and given one point. Piaget has stated that the child learns to solve this problem at about seven or eight years of age.[7] On this task and all others used the determination whether or not a child was successful was made by the evaluator only after a dialogue with him; the child was not rated solely on a yes-or-no answer.

2. The conservation of weight. Piaget believes that this ability is developed at nine or ten years.[8] The student was given two balls of clay and allowed to work with them until he believed that their weights were the same. The examiner then distorted one of the balls. He then asked the student to tell him (without picking up the clay) which portion of the clay weighed more, or if they weighed the same. A correct response placed the student in class II*B* and yielded him two points.

3. The conservation of volume, using the clay just worked with.[9] Piaget has stated that this ability is developed at eleven or twelve years of age.[10] The student was presented two identical containers that contained equal amounts of water and was allowed to work with the volumes until he had convinced himself that the amounts of water were equal. He was then asked whether the distorted ball of clay (from task No. 2) would push the water level up more, whether the nondistorted ball would

[7]Jean Piaget and Bärbel Inhelder, *The Psychology of the Child* (New York, Basic Books, 1969), 99.

[8]*Ibid.*

[9]Jean Piaget, Bärbel Inhelder, and Alina Szeminska, *The Child's Concept of Geometry* (New York, Harper Torchbooks, Harper and Row, 1964), 354.

[10]Piaget and Inhelder, *The Psychology of the Child.*

Success with the conservation-of-volume task is evidence that
early formal thought is present.

push the level up more, or whether the two amounts of clay
would push the levels up equally. Successful completion of the
task confirmed the student's level at IIB, and he was given two
points.

4. *Conservation of volume using two identically shaped cylinders of different weights.* This task involved objects of the
same shape but different weights. This task appealed to the non-

volume conserver who successfully completed task 2 by centering his attention on weight and believing that the levels of the liquid would rise equally because the objects weighed the same. In this task the student was given two metal cylinders of exactly the same size but with an obvious difference in weights. All the foregoing properties of the cylinders were pointed out to the student. He was next presented with two identical cylinders partly filled with water and was allowed to adjust the levels until he was convinced that each tube contained exactly the same amount of water. The student was then asked whether the heavy cylinder would push the level up more, whether the lighter-weight cylinder would push the level up more, or whether the cylinders would push the levels up the same. Successful completion of the task placed the student in class III*A*, and he was awarded three points. If he predicted incorrectly and then explained the event after he saw it, he was classified as II*B* and awarded two points.

5. *Reciprocal implications.*[11] The equipment used resembles a billiard table and a plunger with which a ball can be aimed and shot. The subject was to hit a marker placed on the table, using only one "bank." The subject was questioned about his observations, to determine to what extent he understood that the object could be struck because the angle of incidence equals the angle of reflection.

If the subject realized that the ball traveled in straight lines forming an angle, rather than following a curved path, and if he made general statements that the direction taken by the ball when it left the plunger was determined by the position of the plunger, he was classified as concrete-operational, stage II*A*, and received one point. If he could express the relationship between the position of the plunger and the direction the ball took more accurately by including a reference to the relationship between the inclination of the plunger and that of the line of reflection, he was classified as being concrete-operational,

---

[11]Inhelder and Piaget, *The Growth of Logical Thinking*, 3–19.

stage II*B*, and received two points. If the subject expressed the equivalence of angles between the two directions but thought that this might be a special case and not a general law, he was classified as being formal-operational, stage III*A*, and received three points. If he exhibited confidence in the generality of the law derived—that the angle of incidence equals the angle of reflection—he was classified as being formal operational, stage III*B*, and received four points.

    6. The elimination of contradictions.[12] The student was presented with a small container of water and two wooden blocks. one block was large and heavy and would float; the other block was small and light but sank. The student was asked to predict which block would sink and which would float or whether both blocks would sink or both would float. The prediction was merely a device to involve the examinee in the problem, and no points were awarded for a correct prediction. If the student recognized that a rule probably existed to explain what he saw and that the explanation involved both the weight of the blocks and their volumes, he was ranked II*B* and awarded two points. If the student recognized that the explanation involved the relationship of the volume and weight of the block to an equivalent volume and weight of water, he was rated III*A* and given three points. When the examinee could identify all the variables, order them, derive an hypothesis, test it, and state the results in a logical fashion, he was rated as completely formal-operational, III*B*, and awarded four points.

    We have also used an alternate form of this task. The apparatus for this task consists of a water tank and a selection of objects—a nail, a cork, a rubber stopper, a wooden bead, and two bottles partly filled with water. The larger, heavier bottle floats while the smaller, lighter one sinks. The subject was asked to resolve the apparent contradiction involving the two bottles and derive a law involving the weight and volume of the object compared with the weight and volume of the displaced water.

[12]*Ibid.*, 20–45.

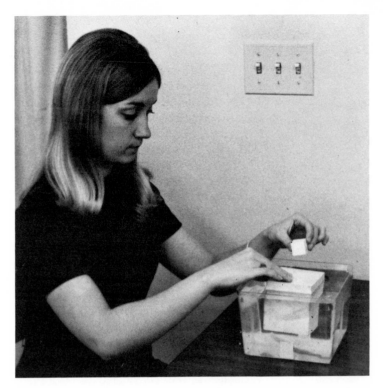

Formal-thought structures are needed to solve the sink-float problem used to identify the ability of a student to be successful with the elimination-of-contradictions task.

If the subject accurately classified objects as sinking or floating objects, but offered multiple explanations relative to floating and sinking, he was classified as being concrete-operational, stage IIA, and received one point. If he stated that there is a general law concerning floating and sinking but did not know the law, and also rejected ideas of absolute weight determining floating and sinking, he was classified as concrete-operational, stage IIB, and received two points. If the subject hypothesized the relationship between weight and volume, but did not verify this hypothesis, he was classified as formal-operational, stage IIIA, and received three points. If he related the weight of the object to the weight of an equivalent volume of water and expressed confidence in the generality of the law, he was classified as formal-operational, stage III*B*, and received four points.

7. *Separation of variables.*[13] In this task the subject was presented with the opportunity to discover the variables affecting how much a rod will bend under varying conditions. The variables available for testing were length, material, cross-sectional area, shape, and amount of weight attached to the end of the rod.

If the subject could categorize and classify the variable factors but did not manipulate the relevant variables, he was classified as concrete-operational, stage II*A*, and received one point. If he exhibited a manipulative scheme, considering many variables, but did not verify the action of one variable, he was classified as concrete-operational, stage II*B*, and received two points. If he attempted to verify his hypotheses and used active searching behavior, attempted to verify the action of the relevant variables, he was considered formal-operational, stage III*A*, and received three points. If he gave a rigorous proof of the action of one variable, he was considered to be formal-operational, stage III*B*, and received four points.[14]

[13]*Ibid.*, 46–66.

[14]Alternate directions for administering the task separation of variables are as follows:

1. The student is shown the apparatus and told that weights are to be added in order to make the rods touch the water. Explain to the student that he may do as many experiments as he likes until he can explain what has to be done to make the various rods touch the water. Typical questions to ask throughout the task:
   a. Do all the rods bend the same amount?
   b. If not, why do the rods not bend the same amount?
   c. What can you do to make the rods bend the same amount?
   d. Can you explain why two rods not alike bend the same amount?
   e. What can you do to prove that the material (or length, or shape, or diameter) of the rod is important in determining how much it will bend?
   f. Which is more important to the bending of a rod, the diameter or the material (or any other combination of variables)?

8. *The exclusion of irrelevant variables.*[15] The examinee was presented with a pendulum whose length could easily be changed and with three different-size weights that could be used for the pendulum bob. He was told to do as many experiments as he needed to, using many different lengths of string and all the various-sized weights until he could explain what he needed to do to make the pendulum go fast or slowly. The variables of string length, angle, weight, and push were also usually pointed out to the student. If the examinee recognized that length was the only relevant variable, that is, if he excluded weight, push, and angle, he was rated II*B* and awarded two points. If he not only excluded the irrelevant variables but also hypothesized a solution to the problem and demonstrated his solution, he was rated III*A* and given three points. If he could

g. How can you prove that your answer is correct?

2. After the exploration the student is asked, "What factors determine the bending of the rods?"

3. The student who simply classifies the rods that bend the most and/or the least into thinker, thinner, longer, shorter, square, round, and so on, is in class II*A* and is awarded one point. This student does not have a combinatorial system to work from that lets him consider proof.

4. The student who classifies but compares two rods using logical multiplication is in class II*B* and is awarded two points. Logical multiplication can be thought of as (thicker) $\times$ (longer) = (thinner) $\times$ (shorter); this learner uses compensation to explain what he sees. The distinguishing factor of a student in either class III*A* or class III*B* is his ability to demonstrate proof by utilizing the "all-things-being-equal" concept. He has a combinatorial system.

5. The student who demonstrates that he can prove that one rod will not bend as much as another by holding, say material, length, and weight (or any combination) constant and experimenting with the diameter is in class III*A* and is awarded three points. Expect this student to try to hold other variables constant and manipulate still others but to fail in some cases. The instructor is permitted to suggest combinations. This learner has the beginning of a combinatorial system.

6. The student who identifies all the variables (weight, length, material, shape, and diameter) and systematically sets about holding all but one constant and tests it, occupies class III*B* and is completely formal-operational; he has a combinatorial system. He is awarded four points.

[15]Inhelder and Piaget, *The Growth of Logical Thinking*, 67–79.

To exclude completely the irrelevant variables found in the simple pendulum problem requires formal thought.

state a general rule about pendulums in such a way that it could be tested, he was rated III*B* and awarded four points.[16]

Determining the Validity of the Formal-Operations Tasks

As has just been explained, we adopted certain of the techniques designed and utilized by Piaget and Inhelder to isolate

[16]Alternative directions for administering the exclusion task:

    1. The subject is shown the apparatus with the following protocol: "This is a pendulum. Have you ever worked with one before? It consists of a string suspended from this stand (the stand is pointed out) and weights that can be hooked on the end of the string like this (the experimenter points out hook on the weight and demonstrates oscillations). I would like you to try to find out what factors affect the

the formal-operational thinker. The question that always plagues an investigator when he uses techniques designed by another is whether those techniques really measure what they purport to measure. Stated in terms of this study, the question would be: Do the conservation of volume, the elimination of contradictions, and the exclusion tasks actually isolate the formal thinker? We had to know.

Earlier we quoted Piaget as having described the formal-operational person as "an individual who thinks beyond the present and forms theories about everything, delighting espe-

length of time it takes the pendulum to swing back and forth. The factors that can be changed are weight, length of string, height of drop, and push (methods of varying these factors are demonstrated). Remember, what you are trying to determine is which of the factors makes a difference in how long it takes the pendulum to swing one complete swing?" (It may be necessary to explain more fully. What is of concern is the period, or length of time, of each swing from one side to the other and back again.)

2. The subject is given a few minutes to explore the variables and their effects on the period.

3. The examiner then asks questions to analyze the subject's understanding of the situation. Possible questions include:

a. What factors affect the time of the swings?
b. Can you prove that length really does have an effect?
c. What about the other factors?
d. Does the height of drop affect the swings?

4. The subject is classified into one of five categories depending upon his actions with the apparatus, his answers to the examiner's questions, and his explanations. The following criteria are used to classify responses:

I   Subject's actions are the cause of the differences. Cannot serial-order.

IIA Can serial-order (example: the longer the string the slower the swings). Cannot serial-order weights.

IIB Can serial-order weight consistently but cannot prove the effect of variables by varying one factor and holding all others constant.

IIIA Can prove the effect of at least one variable but is unable to carry out a valid and systematic test for all variables. This leads to only a partial solution of the problem.

IIIB Can demonstrate proof of the effect of each variable holding all others constant. This leads to a correct and complete solution to the problem.

cially in consideration of that which is not."[17] This individual, then, can form theories or define axioms and then reason without regard to reality. He can fantasize, but his fantasy is always legitimately anchored in logic, even though that logic need not be connected with reality. He can, as has been explained, reason with the "if, then, therefore" construct.

Our attention was then directed to the many fields in which thinking with the foregoing construct represents the field itself. Bruner defines this kind of intellectual operation as "the stock in trade of the logician, the scientist or the abstract thinker."[18] This, then, represented the population from which we could draw to test the validity of the Piagetian tasks we were using. The field of science was immediately ruled out. The reason was obvious; the tasks were too closely allied to science in general and physics in particular. The field of mathematics was also excluded for similar reasons. The population of those engaged in the pursuit of pure logic available to us was not large enough to afford an adequate test population. We were then reminded that the "if, then, therefore" construct was also the stock in trade of the lawyer. He must always find the "if," apply it to the "then," and arrive at the "therefore." All of this must be done in the abstract. We had located our test population—students of law. To survive in the study of law, thinking on an abstract level is essential. The question remained whether or not our task would show the students to be formal-operational.

The aid of two law schools was enlisted. One had a complete resident population, and the other had a predominantly working, night-school population. We randomly sampled the first- and third-year classes (a total of forty-four students) on the conservation of volume, the elimination of contradictions, and the exclusion principle. The results are shown in Table 6. The numbers shown on the top horizontal have the same meaning

---

[17]Piaget, *Psychology of Intelligence.*

[18]Jerome Bruner, *The Process of Education* (New York, Vintage Books, 1960), 37.

as before, that is, IIA, IIB, IIIA, and IIIB. The highest score possible on the conservation of volume using clay was IIB.

Table 6. Scores of Performances of Law Students on Three Formal-Operational Tasks

$(N = 44)$

Task	IIA	IIB	IIIA	IIIB
Conservation of volume using clay	7	37		
Elimination of contradictions		6	15	23
Exclusion	6	7	12	19

Interpreting the data in Table 6 is essential to making statements about the validity of the tasks to isolate formal-operational thinkers. Thirty-seven of forty-four subjects (84%) scored the maximum on the first task. Furthermore, the IIIB scores were the greatest numbers of any for tasks two and three. In other words, there were more IIIB thinkers (completely formal-operational) in our sample than any other level. With that result we agreed that anyone who reached IIIA or IIIB would be called formal-operational. Using that criterion, we determined that thirty-eight of forty-four subjects (86.5 per cent) were formal-operational on the elimination of contradictions, and that thirty-one of forty-four subjects (71 per cent) reached formal operations on the exclusion task. Since these two tasks isolate formal thinkers, the data could be combined to give a general notion of their ability to isolate the formal thinker. When that is done (69 divided by 88), a total achievement of the law students tested is 78.5 per cent. If the data from the conservation of volume are added (106 divided by 132), a total of 81 per cent emerges. (Remember that a person could achieve only IIB on that particular volume conservation.) In other words, the body we *defined* as formal-operational achieved 81 per cent on those tasks that purported to measure formal-operational thought. We concluded that we had tasks that would allow us to isolate the formal-operational thinker.

A further step was taken to determine the factorial validity of all the tasks we had used in assessing formal thought by using the statistical technique of principal-components analysis. This technique is basically a multiple-regression procedure that involves correlation of factors or components measured by the tasks. Since the tasks of conservation of solid amount, conservation of weight, and conservation of volume using clay are all intended to measure the same thing—concrete-operational thinking—scores on these tasks should reflect similar trends.

The tasks of conservation of volume in which two identically shaped cylinders of different weights, reciprocal implications, elimination of contradictions, separation of variables, and exclusion of irrelevant variables are intended to measure levels of formal-operational thinking. It would, therefore, be expected that subject scores on these tasks would also reflect similar trends. The results of these analyses will be detailed in Chapter 8. At this point it suffices to say that the tasks do indeed have factorial validity. The concrete-task scores exhibit similar trends and correlate highly with the one principal component, while the formal-task scores also exhibit similar trends but correlate closely with a different principal component.

To continue our study of the relationship of curriculum experiences and intellectual development, research was needed to link the attainment or actuation of formal-operational thinking to curriculum experiences. Since junior high school students have the physiological maturation prerequisite to the development of formal operations, research could be designed to evaluate the influence of curriculum experiences on the attainment of this level of thinking. The research described in Chapter 5 was designed to compare the influence of inquiry-oriented science programs on the actuation of propositional logic or formal-operational-thinking ability.

5. Curriculum Experiences and Movement from Concrete-Operational Thought

F. Elizabeth Friot

According to Piaget, if the student has the prerequisite physiological maturity, his logical thought processes change significantly when he is permitted to *interact* with objects, events, and situations in his environment.[1] The goal of intellectual development, therefore, can best be attained by providing those situations in which the learner has the opportunity to interact with whatever he is to be taught—of course, with his safety in mind.

The Curricula and Teachers

How can the goal of intellectual development be reached by students? In what school settings can those interactions that produce intellectual development be facilitated? Because of

[1]For justification of this statement, see student-teacher dialogues in Inhelder and Piaget, *The Growth of Logical Thinking.*

what our research into science teaching and learning in the elementary school had shown us (reported in Chapters 2 and 3), we hypothesized that when junior high school science experiences were provided that centered around and demanded student investigations intellectual development would be affected. The first task of this research, therefore, was to identify junior high school science courses that emphasized student investigations. Several were found. The courses have as their primary objective the development of learner ability to solve problems; they also emphasize experimentation, which means that the learners become involved in the interaction of ideas and objects, operations specified by Piaget as essential to the development of formal-operational thought. The three courses identified are "Introductory Physical Science" (IPS),[2] "Time, Space, and Matter," (TSM),[3] and "Investigating the Earth"—the Earth Science Curriculum Project—(ESCP).[4] These courses are taught at the eighth- and ninth-grade levels and can be properly labeled as of the "inquiry kind," which means, of course, that they emphasize student involvement through investigations.

The IPS curriculum is oriented toward the over-all goal of developing understanding, through investigation, of the structure of matter. No attempt is made to cover all the topics commonly found in junior high school physical-science courses. Rather, an effort was made to identify those investigations which would be of most value to learners as they developed their logical-thought processes.

The TSM course is a study of the matter found on earth and elsewhere in the solar system and the time-space relationship of this matter. Since the printed material is minimal—con-

---

[2]IPS. Group, *Introductory Physical Science* (Englewood Cliffs, N.J., Prentice-Hall, 1967).

[3]Secondary School Science Project, *Time, Space, and Matter* (St. Louis, Mo., Webster Division, McGraw-Hill Book Company, Inc., 1966).

[4]"Investigating the Earth," Earth Science Curriculum Project (ed. by Raymond E. Bisque and Robert L. Heller), (Boston, Houghton, Mifflin, and Co., 1973).

sisting of nine picture folios and a series of reading pamphlets—the learner *must perform investigations* if he is to find solutions to the problems suggested by the teacher. As the student keeps daily records of his observations and investigations, he writes his own book.

The designers of the ESCP course determined a selection of topics representative of the earth sciences and designed investigations to amplify the material presented. The course is more content-oriented than are the other two.

The teachers working with the classes involved in this research were selected by their administrators and the researchers as competent to teach the courses assigned to them. The administrators were acquainted with both the teachers and the curricula assigned to them. Each teacher of the inquiry curricula had received instruction in teaching that kind of curriculum.

An important part of this research was the control groups. Included was one class at each grade level whose science experience was essentially reading from a textbook (the traditional method). The teachers of those groups had not received instruction in the teaching of inquiry science courses. The methodology used in the traditional classes was of the traditional recitation-demonstration kind.

The Students

The seven classes involved in the research were distributed among the experimental groups (TSM, IPS, and ESCP) and the control groups (general science, traditional) according to the scheme shown in Table 7. The number of students involved was 210.

Each student enrolled in certain required subjects and certain elective subjects. There is no reason to believe that any one combination of subjects existing at the institutions moved a student into formal logic any better than any other combination of subjects. The subjects required of all students were English, social science, mathematics, and science.

Table 7. Distribution of Eighth- and Ninth-Grade Students Among the Curricula Used

Grade Level	Course Title	Number of Students
8	IPS	30
	ESCP	30
	TSM	30
	Traditional	30
9	IPS	30
	ESCP	30
	Traditional	30

Collecting the Data

To evaluate student movement from concrete thought into formal thought, each of the 210 students was interviewed twice—in September, 1969, and in April, 1970—with six Piagetian tasks. The particular tasks used, which were described in Chapter 4, were:

1. The conservation of solid amount (this task was used to establish clearly that the student was concrete-operational)
2. The conservation of volume, using two identically shaped metal cylinders of different weights
3. Reciprocal implications
4. The elimination of contradictions (the alternate form described in Chapter 4)
5. The separation of variables
6. The exclusion of irrelevant variables

From the work of Inhelder and Piaget[5] we made the assumption that *a learner will not respond correctly to the tasks (with the exception of the conservation of solid amount) until he has at*

---

[5]Inhelder and Piaget, *The Growth of Logical Thinking.*

least entered the formal-operational stage. The repeated use of the tasks, therefore, does not lead to spurious results. The rating that each childreceived on each of the tasks was based more on the reasons he gave for responding as he did than on the answer he gave. Even with that assurance, to eliminate the teachers' temptation to teach the solution to the tasks between the September and April evaluations, they did not view or participate in the testing.

The data from the administration of the tasks were then compared for individuals, classes, courses of study, and grade levels. The hypothesis tested, stated in null form, was that students who are exposed to an inquiry-kind of science course showed no statistically significant gains in the attainment of formal-operational thought when compared with students taking a traditional lecture-demonstration course.

The Results

Tables 8 and 9 summarize the testing data. Since there were differences in the pretest scores of the various groups, the data were analyzed in terms of the gain in score, that is, the posttest score minus the pretest score. In some cases the gains in conservation of solid amount and conservation of volume were small compared with the gains in the other tasks; that finding reflects the fact that many individuals conserved in those areas on the pretest and thus showed no gain.

According to the Piagetian theory one of the factors that controls intellectual development is maturation (see Chapter 1) not only of the nervous system but also of the entire body. That tenet is supported by the fact that each group posted gains in incidences of formal thought between pretests and posttests. The fact that gains were made on each task—the gains did not follow a random pattern—further substantiates this conclusion. The fact that a stable pattern of intellectual growth was found lends credibility to the basic operational tenet of this research; that is, logical thinking can be evaluated.

Table 8. Pretest and Posttest Scores on the Six Piagetian Tasks for Control and Experimental Groups

Group	Control	ESCP	IPS	TSM	Control	ESCP	IPS
Grade	8	8	8	8	9	9	9
Pretest	312	288	278	301	265	308	319
Posttest	382	318	375	433	335	427	465
Gain	70	30	97	132	70	119	146

Table 9. Gain in Piagetian Task Scores for Control and Experimental Groups, Classified by Task

Group	Control	ESCP	IPS	TSM	Control	ESCP	ISP
Grade	8	8	8	8	9	9	9
Conservation of solid amount	1	−1	−2	2	2	1	8
Conservation of volume	10	10	17	23	4	23	11
Reciprocal Reciprocal implications	27	27	23	42	18	17	38
Elimination of contradictions	21	1	8	38	7	23	46
Separation of variables	5	10	24	25	16	11	35
Exclusion	1	1	19	36	19	19	27

The scores for the individuals in each group were compared for each task, and the numerical differences in the scores (posttest minus pretest) were used to compute the F values used in Table 10. The hypothesis was tested at the 0.10 level of significance. The goal of the study was not to accept the null hypothesis if it was actually false. To do so would impede the further development and implementation of inquiry science courses. Since some of the achievements of inquiry courses are not readily evaluated on a numerical basis, labeling these courses as ineffective because the tests used could not adequately evaluate the achievement of the students would be a serious error. The reverse, rejecting the null hypothesis when it was actually true, would do far less harm. This decision was made with the full realization that the treatment might be given too much emphasis.

Table 10.

F Values and Indication of Significance at 0.10 Level for All Combinations of Courses and Groups Available

Hypothesis	F Value Obtained	F-Table Value	Indication of Significance	In Favor of
Control 8– TSM 8	3.57	2.84	Yes	TSM
Control 8– IPS 8	1.05	2.84	No	Neither
Control 8– ESCP 8	−7.4	2.84	Yes	Control
IPS 8– TSM 8	21	2.84	Yes	TSM
ESCP 8– IPS 8	41	2.84	Yes	IPS
ESCP 8– TSM 8	57	2.84	Yes	TSM
Control 9– IPS 9	24	2.84	Yes	IPS
Control 9– ESCP 9	22	2.84	Yes	ESCP
ESCP 9– IPS 9	4.9	2.84	Yes	IPS
IPS 8– IPS 9	26	2.84	Yes	IPS 9
ESCP 8– ESCP 9	147	2.84	Yes	ESCP 9

The operational levels of the eight- and ninth-grade learners as indicated by their scores on the pretest and posttest were found. A score of twelve or below indicated concrete operations, scores of thirteen or fourteen indicated a transitional stage and a score of fifteen or greater indicated formal operations. The results are shown in Table 11.

An Interpretation

The data in Table 11 show that 82 per cent of the learners were concrete-operational at the time of the pretest and that 44 per cent were concrete-operational as measured by the posttest. The corresponding figures for formal-operational learners showed an increase from 6 per cent at the time of the pretest and 40 per cent at the time of the posttest. Most of the gain in formal thought, however, is produced by the eighth-grade TSM and the ninth-grade IPS courses; those groups account for 49 of the 84 formal thinkers—57.5 per cent. If the 60 students comprising those groups were removed from consideration, the population in the research would decrease to 150, and the number of formal thinkers would drop to 35—23.3 per cent as opposed to the 40 per cent shown in Table 11. Those percentages—40 per cent as opposed to 23.3 per cent—give some indication of the importance of inquiry-centered learning to intellectual development. Both the IPS and TSM courses are educational experiences that emphasize a "hands-on" approach with respect to materials and an environment that nurtures student inquiries. The ESCP course purports to be of the inquiry kind; the data in this research, however, do not reveal it as being as effective in producing increased intellectual operations as the other programs. We hypothesize that the content of that course is largely based upon formal operational concepts. We shall return to the formal-concept notion in Chapter 9.

Note that only seven students in the TSM and ninth-grade IPS groups were rated as concrete-operational on the posttest.

Grade Level and Curriculum	Concrete Operations		Transitional Stage		Formal Operations	
	Pretest	Posttest	Pretest	Posttest	Pretest	Posttest
Eighth-grade General science	22	13	7	6	1	10
Eighth-grade ESCP	25	24	4	4	1	2
Eighth-grade IPS	27	17	2	6	1	7
Eighth-grade TSM	23	5	1	2	2	24
Ninth-grade General science	28	20	1	5	1	5
Ninth-grade IPS	22	2	5	3	3	25
Ninth-grade ESCP	25	11	2	8	3	11
Total	172	92	26	34	12	84
Percentage of total	82	44	12	16	6	40

Table 11. Operational Level of Eighth- and Ninth-Grade Learners

Science activities that demand that students have "hands-on" experiences with materials can move them into the formal-operational stage.

Again, when those two troups (60 students) were removed from consideration, 85 of the remaining 150 students were found to be concrete-operational (53.1 per cent). That means that 46.9 per cent of eighth- and ninth-graders have entered the period of formal thought or are making the transition to it. Since the Piagetian model states that the formal period is entered between eleven and fifteen years of age (see Chapter 4), the students in this study obviously do not meet those criteria. The junior high school in which this research was carried out was not atypical in any way. We feel, therefore, that the following question is in order: Is the educational environment of the learners in our schools deficient in some way that impedes the full intellectual development of learners? The data provided here by the TSM and IPS groups demonstrate that children in the age bracket specified by Piaget can be led to develop formal thought.

The study showed that the effectiveness of the curricula with respect to changing the operational level of the learners varied according to grade level. The curriculum that caused the most change in the operational level of the eighth-grade learners was TSM—indeed, it was the only curriculum that caused a significant change in the learners' developmental level. The ninth-grade learners' development was significantly affected by both IPS and ESCP, but those who worked with the IPS curriculum made the most progress. Therefore, if a decision was made that eighth- and ninth-grade learners should study the earth and physical sciences, the most effective combination of courses would be TSM for the eighth-graders and IPS for the ninth-graders. While ESCP did cause significant changes in the operational level of the ninth-graders, it was not as effective as IPS, and it was not even as effective as was the control group at the eighth-grade level.

This study points out several very important things. The most important is that learners can be moved from concrete operations to formal operations by virtue of their school experiences. The defining of school experiences that best do this should receive our prime attention. The evaluation techniques used, modeled after developmental tasks described by Piaget, *allow us to discriminate among curricula on the basis of their effectiveness in helping the learners become formal-operational.* This topic is treated in detail in Chapter 9. We are able, therefore, not only to move learners to higher operational levels but also to ascertain the most effective curricula to use for this task.

Throughout this chapter percentages of students occupying the various Piagetian levels were given. Those percentages of course apply to only the eighth and ninth grades. Does the ability to use formal thought develop during the secondary school years? The research described in Chapter 6 attempts to answer that question.

6. The Operational Levels of Secondary School Students

John W. Renner and Donald G. Stafford

The formal-operational concept is rich with implications for the secondary school curriculum. The diagraming of sentences, for example, requires the student to isolate and separate variables; the mastering of interchangeable measuring systems requires the conservation of volume; and the presentation of the facts of a political campaign of the past and isolation of the reasons why certain events took place as a result of that campaign requires that the learner be able to eliminate contradictions. The general notion that the foregoing kinds of abstract thinking require formal operational thought puts an even more penetrating spotlight on the secondary school. The concept of the atom, for example—because it is a mental model—is an abstraction and requires formal operational thought.

The Problem

When one considers the entire secondary school curriculum, the identification of those learnings that require formal thought is not difficult; many of those learnings are also considered necessary to a secondary school education. To date, however, no comprehensive study of the secondary school population's ability to utilize abstract thought (formal operations) has been conducted. Piaget has said that the adolescent enters the formal period between eleven and twelve years of age[1] and reaches "an equilibrium point at about fourteen to fifteen years."[2] But do those age ranges apply to the students populating American secondary schools? We decided to find out.

The Population

The population that was sampled consisted of the students in grades seven through twelve in the public schools of Oklahoma. The state was divided into several sections, the criterion being how the citizens of each region supported themselves: for example, in agriculture, ranching, mining, and industry. Also included in our sampling procedures was the urban-rural-ghetto concentration of the population. Schools were randomly selected from the identified sections of the state, and students were randomly selected from each school.

The Procedures

During the 1970–71 school year (between September and March) 588 students in grades seven through twelve from twenty-five schools were interviewed; only five interviewers participated,[3] and approximately 50 per cent of the sample was interviewed by one person. All the interviewers were trained by the same person in interviewing techniques. The size of the sample by grades was:

[1]Piaget, *Psychology of Intelligence*, 123.
[2]Inhelder and Piaget, *The Growth of Logical Thinking*, 335.
[3]The interviewers were Jill De Spain and Martha Nell Dodson, Oklahoma City Public Schools, Larry McKinney, Oklahoma State Department of Education; Joe W. McKinnon; and John W. Renner.

Seventh grade: 96 students
Eighth grade: 108 students
Ninth grade: 94 students
Tenth grade: 94 students
Eleventh grade: 99 students
Twelfth grade: 97 students

Each of the interviewees was assigned Tasks 1, 2, 3, 4, 6 (Part One), and 8, described in Chapter 4. Tasks 1 and 2 were included to establish that the interviewee was concrete-operational. The other four tasks were, as described in Chapter 4, at the Class III (formal-operational) level. The student was given a score on each task, according to the scoring procedures described in Chapter 4. The rating of each student, however, was influenced at least as much by his dialogue with the interviewer, his explanations of what he perceived about the tasks, and the procedures he used in solving the problem as it was by his exact answers. During the exclusion task, for example (task 8), if the student held the length of the string constant and systematically tested all three weights and then changed the string's length and again tested each weight, the interviewer took those actions as evidence that the student was *probably* separating variables. The score assigned to each interviewee was not a pure analytical determination but reflected the human factor.

The data from each interview were recorded on a form similar to the one shown below. The maximum number of points that could be earned on each task is shown in parenthesis following the name of each task; that number is also placed beneath the particular column that represents the maximum level a student could achieve on that task. The maximum score the student could achieve during the interview was sixteen. If, for example, a student was rated II*B* on the elimination-of-contradictions task, he was awarded two points (not four) on that task. On tasks 2 through 6 no interviewee was rated less II*A if* he satisfactorily completed the first task (solid amount conservation).

School_____Date_____

Name_____Grade_____

Date of Birth_____

Task	IIA	IIB	IIIA	IIIB
Conservation of solid amount	(1)			
Conservation of weight		(2)		
Conservation of volume using clay		(2)		
Conservation of volume			(3)	
Elimination of contradictions				(4)
Exclusion of irrelevant variables				(4)

Evaluator_____

The Data

The distribution of scores for the entire sample is shown in Table 12.[4] Those interviewees receiving a score of five or below are at best early concrete-operational. (One wonders how the eight interviewees, in grades ten through twelve reached senior high school (or that the twelfth-grader was about to graduate.) Many combinations of scores would result in a total score of between six and eleven and not include a single IIIA rating. That group was rated concrete-operational. By successfully completing all tasks, the students reached a score of fourteen. From our frame of reference that was the minimum achievement necessary to be called formal-operational. So far scores twelve and thirteen have not been accounted for. That group of students demonstrated more intellectual development than the group scoring eleven and below, and so they were more than concrete-operational; still they were not formal-operational. That group was labeled transitional.

[4]John W. Renner and Don G. Stafford, *Teaching Science in the Secondary School*, (1st ed., New York, Harper and Row, 1972), Appendix A.

	Grade						Totals
Score	7 (N=96)	8 (N=108)	9 (N=94)	10 (N=94)	11 (N=99)	12 (N=97)	(N=588)
0-5	5	3	4	4	3	1	20
6	8	5	5	6	5	3	32
7	11	20	10	9	6	10	66
8	23	16	12	19	16	3	89
9	13	13	12	9	14	15	76
10	15	20	19	11	13	19	97
11	5	7	16	11	11	13	63
12	8	9	4	10	13	6	50
13	5	9	3	5	6	9	37
14	2	3	6	5	4	6	26
15	0	1	1	3	5	8	18
16	1	2	2	2	3	4	14

Table 12. Distribution of Scores

In presenting data such as those in Table 12 we are fully cognizant that we have deviated from the manner in which Inhelder and Piaget present their findings. They normally present portions of dialogues with individual students and so demonstrate the thinking patterns of the age group under consideration. Our research was aimed at applying the exacting clinical procedures of the Geneva group to a large sample of the secondary school population. We believe that dialogues of the kind that Inhelder and Piaget held with those students upon whom they reported were held with every student in the 588-student sample that we utilized. Rather than report those dialogues, however, we report in Table 12 the judgments made by the five interviewers a total of 588 times. Our purpose was to paint a picture of the prevalence of the several operational abilities described by Piaget and not to present data to demonstrate to the reader that the several operational states exist. The reader interested in how and why Piaget established the several operational levels is urged to read his *Psychology of Intelligence* (cited in the first footnote of this chapter).

Reducing the Data

When the four categories just described (early concrete-operational, fully concrete-operational, transitional, and formal-operational) are employed, the data shown in Table 12 reduce to those shown in Table 13.

Table 13. Summary of the Data

Score	Classification	Number of Students
0–5	Early concrete-operational	20
6–11	Fully concrete-operational	423
12–13	Transitional	87
14–16	Formal-operational	58

Of the 58 students achieving formal operational status, only those scoring sixteen could be called fully formal-operational. That number is 14 of 588—2.4 per cent. Equally important, if the size of the early concrete operational group is added to the fully concrete operational group, this latter percentage becomes 75.3. In other words, 75.3 per cent of the students in the secondary schools are, at best, concrete-operational—a stage of intellectual development which Piaget's data have told him children begin to leave about eleven years of age and from which they have emerged by age fifteen. The students in the sample studied in this research were between twelve and nineteen years of age.

Earlier in this chapter the procedure for identifying the concrete-operational thinkers—those scoring eleven or less—was described. An interviewee could, for example, score III*B* on the last task (exclusion), II*A* on the contradictions task and the second volume-conservation task, II*B* on tasks 2 and 3, and II*A* on task 1 and still score only eleven even though he scored III*B* on the last task. Our procedure for handling data does not point out the III*B* this interviewee scored, as Piaget's interview reports would show. After considering the large amount of data being handled and the purposes for doing the research, the decision was made to rate any student who scored eleven or below, *regardless of how he did it*, concrete-operational. The researchers are aware that they have deviated from Piaget's established practices, but, as was described earlier, those practices were utilized by each interviewer in making judgments about the score to be awarded a student.

Table 14 shows, by grades, the distribution of students scoring eleven or below on the six tasks; those data point out the location of the nonformal operational thinkers in the secondary school.

An Interpretation

The data shown in Table 14 are devastating when secondary school curricula are compared to them. Consider the tenth

Table 14. Distribution of Students

Grade	Sample Size	Number scoring 11 or Below	Percentage of the Sample
7	96	80	83
8	108	83	77
9	94	77	82
10	94	68	73
11	99	70	71
12	97	64	66

grade. During that year the student normally makes his first contact with Euclidean geometry. Finding a better example of a secondary school course that requires more formal operational thinking than does Euclidean geometry is difficult. Yet, if this sample is representative, 73 per cent of today's tenth-graders are not capable of formal-operational thought. Several years ago the Biological Sciences Curriculum Study developed a tenth-grade biology course that has its roots in biochemistry. The first requirement for understanding such a course is to have a well-developed concept of the atom. The structure of the atom, which is today (and always has been) accepted, is an abstract mental model that requires formal thinking. The fact remains that 73 per cent of today's tenth-graders are not capable of such abstract thinking.

Examples need not be confined to mathematics and science for the data shown in Table 14 to be disturbing. Earlier in this chapter the task of diagraming sentences was referred to as requiring formal-operational thinking. That grammatical jewel is usually taught to seventh-graders—all of them. Yet 83 per cent of those seventh-graders cannot think at the level necessary to comprehend what is being done.

What do students do to survive in a system that hour after hour requires them to cope with situations they cannot begin to handle? They have only two choices—memorize or cheat. But by the way the system rewards them, they not only survive but are applauded for "how much they know." Teachers have been heard to say over and over, "They're getting it." They have actually convinced themselves that, just because a child repeats something on an examination, he is "getting it." How absurd! What that teacher is really saying is, "The students are beginning to memorize what I want them to, and their minds are beginning to resemble mine." Little wonder that 66 per cent of the graduating seniors are still concrete-operational.

Foreign languages have long been a colossal failure in our educational system; the data shown in Table 14 are helpful in finding out why. Foreign languages are normally taught from a grammatical—not a speaking—frame of reference. A theoretical grammatical structure is an abstraction that requires formal-operational thought. Examining the percentage of concrete operational thinkers in nearly any grade of the secondary school will demonstrate that putting there the teaching of a theoretical grammatical structure (such as the Latin-grammar structure of English) will fail.

Foreign languages have been remarkably successful in the elementary schools, high schools, and colleges when taught as a vehicle for verbal communication. That is not surprising, because speech is at best a concrete-operational act wherein words are invented to explain situations, name objects, and describe events. Witness the early age at which speech is learned. Schools, however, manage to take the language and introduce its formal-operational aspects to a mainly nonformal-operational group and are then surprised that achievement lags, and interest and motivation vanish. The data shown in Table 14 explain why and also demonstrate how naïve schools, teachers, and particularly the leadership have been.

A Question

Physics is normally a twelfth-grade subject, and there is little doubt that physics is primarily a formal-operational subject. Yet 66 per cent of today's twelfth-graders are still concrete-operational. There is, in addition, another factor that must be considered: *Not all twelfth-graders enroll in physics.* In fact, less than 15 per cent do. Are 66 per cent of those students who enroll in such courses as senior English, trigonometry, fourth-year French, and physics (all of which are taught at the formal level) also concrete-operational? We do not know. That question needs to be answered before the results of this study can be implemented. The question for research might be something like this: What kinds of thinkers do the various subjects in the secondary school attract?

Gains Made Toward Formal Operations

The data shown in Table 15 present an over-all picture of the operational level of secondary school students and shed some light on where gains are made toward formal-operational thinking.

Table 15. Function of Age

Grade	Mean Score	Mean Gain Made Within Each Grade
7	9.07	
		0.38
8	9.45	
		0.21
9	9.66	
		0.06
10	9.72	
		0.23
10	9.95	
		0.79
12	10.74	

When all scores for each grade were lumped together, no group achieved the maximum concrete-operational score of eleven. From an arithmetical-average point of view the entire sample is concrete-operational. The data shown in Table 15 clearly demonstrate that the movement through the concrete-operational stage and toward the formal stage is a function of age. That point will be more thoroughly investigated later in this book.

The column in Table 15 headed "Mean Gain Made Within Each Grade" suggests some interesting interpretations.[5] The maximum gain between any two grades is the 0.79 gain made between grades eleven and twelve; perhaps that once again shows the relationship between age and movement toward formal operations. Note that no linear pattern is associated with the mean gain from grade to grade; there is, however, a pattern. The gain from eighth to ninth grade is less than the gain from seventh to eighth grade but greater than the gain from ninth to tenth grade. That suggests that the least important year with respect to gain in logical-reasoning ability is the tenth year, although, as we shall show later, the slope becomes slightly positive here. Reflect back to some earlier remarks about the tenth-grade curriculum. Is there a relationship between that curriculum and the minimal gains made toward the acquisition of formal-operational thinking? Is the curriculum of grades seven, through ten related to the fact that the gain in the acquisition of logical thought is less each succeeding year until the end of grade ten? These are interesting questions on which to speculate.

The students in the sample gained in acquisition of those reasoning abilities which moved them toward formal thought during the eleventh grade and twelfth grades. Is that a function of the curriculum and experience provided by the school, or is it merely due to the fact that the students are older? Obviously, much research needs to be done before such questions can be

[5]It must be borne in mind that all measurements were made within the year. The gain from grade nine to grade ten is really the gain from within grade nine to within grade ten. Since all students were treated alike, however, the questions asked with respect to the effectiveness of grade to grade is still valid.

answered. But questions such as the foregoing must be asked. The curriculum of the secondary school has for years reflected what "experts" thought should be there. The data in this research clearly demonstrate that such a procedure is not producing the best results. The time has come when the curriculum should be selected because it matches the intellectual needs of the learners and not because of tradition or because some pressure group put it there. Schools are for children — not for well-meaning but ill-informed adults.

Other research done on as massive a scale as this research, which would enable comparisons to be made, is not readily available. One comparison can be made, but it must be carefully interpreted. Kohlberg and Gilligan report:

. . . the percentage of 265 persons at various ages showing clear formal-operational reasoning at the pendulum task is as follows:
Age ten to fifteen: 45 per cent.
Age sixteen to twenty: 53 per cent.[6]

Clearly, the percentage of formal-operational thought cited in the foregoing research is higher than that found in the present research. The research quoted above was done with only one formal-operational task, and the population background is not known. The present research contained *three* tasks upon which every interviewee could demonstrate formal thought, and the population was randomly selected. Even considering the foregoing differences, both research projects show a remarkably low attainment of formal-operational thought. Kohlberg and Gilligan go on to state that, between the ages of twenty-one to thirty, 65 per cent of the sample demonstrated formal thought on the pendulum task (exclusion). Furthermore, between the ages of forty-five to fifty, that percentage fell to 57.[7] They made

[6]Lawrence Kohlberg and Carol Gilligan, "The Adolescent as Philosopher: The Discovery of the Self in a Postconventional World," *Daedalus: Journal of the American Academy of Arts and Sciences*, Vol. 100, No. 4 (Fall, 1971), 1051–86 (hereafter cited as *Daedalus*).
[7]*Ibid.*, 1065.

the generalization that "a large portion of Americans never develop the capacity for abstract thought."[8] The present research and that reported by Kohlberg and Gilligan clearly demonstrate that a problem exists within our society with respect to cultivating the ability to think formally. When one considers the fact that *each* person in this country at the age of graduation from high school begins to particiapte in decisions of government, through voting, which, if done properly, requires a high level of abstract hypothetical reasoning, he begins to wonder how we have fared as well as we have to this point in history. It is imperative that hypothetical (formal operational) reasoning be developed to its highest level possible by our educational program for *every* student. The role the school can play in promoting the acquisition of formal operations will be examined in Chapter 9.

There are clearly several other variables in the present research that may have an influence upon the acquisition of formal operational thought. The variable of age as a possibly significant one has already been alluded to. Factors such as sex and size of school need to be examined closely to see what impact they have upon an individual's attainment of formal operations. The significance of such variables will next be examined.

The data in Table 15 were used to produce Figure 12. Although the data were organized by grade, the increase in age from grade to grade is approximately one year. A definite increase in the ability to perform on the six Piagetian tasks used is evident. The shape of the curve indicates a decreasing slope (growth) in junior high school and an increasing slope (growth) in senior high school. What was said earlier about grade ten should be reviewed. Is the positive slope the result of the curriculum or the fact that the learner is getting older?) One would be tempted to look for a difference in the junior high and senior high school programs to explain the growth curve in Figure 12. A partial answer can be provided, however, by simply regroup-

---

[8]*Ibid.*

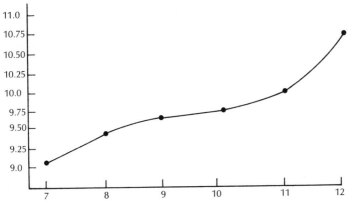

Fig. 12. Age versus task performance

ing the students on the basis of age without regard to grade level. The result, shown in Figure 13, indicates that the change in over-all score is essentially constant with age.

If one makes the assumption that the ability to use abstract propositional reasoning remains linear, as in the case of the male sample in Figure 13 and then extends the curve (extrapolates) to the average age at which men would make an average score close to sixteen, the age would be almost forty years. (The notion that intellectual development continues to near age forty was, in fact, supported by the early Greek philosophers.) Perhaps this increased intellectual power explains why many teachers continue to see new relationships and old relationships in their subject more clearly. If this is the case, teachers need to be constantly aware of this difference in their intellectual powers and those of students. The assumption, "If I can understand this relationship, so could the students," is not valid. Teachers must keep the students' level in mind while planning activities to develop a concept rather than basing the teaching procedure on their own intellectual capabilities.

Sex and Scores on the Piaget Tasks

Figure 13 reveals a surprising but pronounced difference in the over-all level of performance on the six tasks between boys and

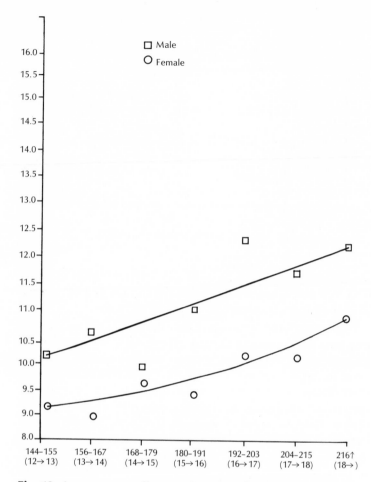

Fig. 13. Average over-all scores by vertical column by age groups (months and, in parentheses, years)

girls at every age level. This difference is statistically significant at a high level of confidence (0.05 or better). We cannot propose an explanation for this difference. It is interesting, however, to note the difference in the curves. The male curve is linear (constant increase), with some data points variable. (A much greater variability of male performance in general compared to female was noted by the investigators.) The female curve gently but definitely increases. If one assumes that the female curve remains constant, extrapolation of the two curves would indicate an intersection at approximately twenty-two years of age, with an average score of thirteen—the transitional range.

An internal examination of the sex-related differences in the total scores on the tasks reveals some interesting patterns. Figure 14 shows the number of students by sex who could perform the task at the lowest (most concrete) level of response. These data reveal that, if one recorded a simple yes (1) or no (0) for each student who could perform the task without regard to the type of reasoning used, the difference in over-all male-female performance is negligible.

Figure 15 shows that the basis for the males' significantly superior performance is due to points gained for a greater frequency of formal-operational-level explanations. As the tasks

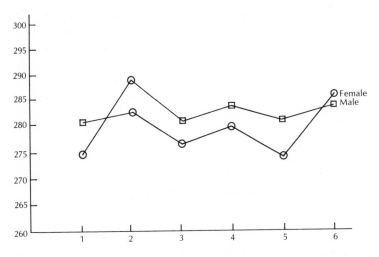

Fig. 14. Number of students scoring at least one (1) on the six tasks (horizontal numbers are task numbers)

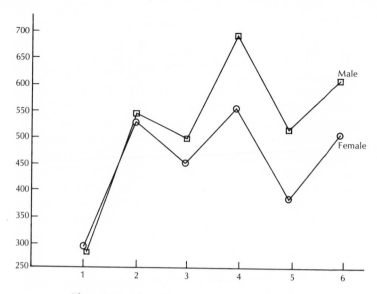

Fig. 15. Total scores of all students by tasks

increased in degree of complexity and/or level of hypothetical reasoning required for their solution, the curves continue to separate, although they retain the same shape.

Is it possible that girls need a different set of experiences in school from those that boys need? Perhaps the secondary school experiences are already so different for male and female students that the variances in reasoning ability results. Or could it be (and we tremble at the repercussions of this suggestion) that, contrary to popular thinking, males mature intellectually (not necessarily socially) earlier than girls? Furthermore, is what teachers are calling superior academic ability in girls really their ability to conform to teacher wishes?

Intellectual Development and School Size

Now to a question that is probably as controversial as the sex comparison; What size of school appears to do the best job of helping students develop intellectually? To approach this question, the sample was subdivided on the basis of school enrollment: (small 51 to 273, medium 274 to 713, and large 714 to 2,382). Table 16 summarized data regarding sex, school, size, age, and average total score.[9]

Table 16. Mean Responses of Total Group as Related to Piagetian Developmental Thought Processes, Task 6, in Regard to School Size, Sex, and Age*

| | *Size of School* | | | | | |
| | *Small* | | *Medium* | | *Large* | |
Sex	*Male*	*Female*	*Male*	*Female*	*Male*	*Female*
Age, Months						
145–154	1.71	1.57	1.64	1.60	2.25	1.42
155–164	2.22	2.00	1.20	1.38	1.68	1.63
165–174	1.38	1.29	1.75	1.12	1.83	1.60
175–184	1.20	2.23	1.80	1.66	1.90	2.50
185–194	2.14	1.46	2.00	1.94	1.66	1.37
195–204	2.64	1.53	2.05	1.82	4.00	2.50
205–214	2.13	1.33	2.26	2.00	3.00	2.20
215–224	1.45	1.60	2.14	1.00	4.00	2.80

*Between size	d.f. $= (2,573)$	$F = 5.47$ sig. at P 0.001
Between sex	d.f. $= (1,573)$	$F = 10.50$ sig. at P 0.001
Between age	d.f. $= (7,573)$	$F = 3.03$ sig. at P 0.01
Interactions:		
Size $\times$ sex	d.f. $= (2,573)$	$F = 5.00$ sig. at P 0.001
Size $\times$ age	d.f. $= (14,573)$	$F = 1.83$ sig. at P 0.05
Sex $\times$ age	d.f. $= (7,573)$	$F = 1.44$ n.s.
All variables	d.f. $= (14,573)$	$F = 0.69$ n.s.

Analysis of the over-all data in the table reveals a definite and statistically significant difference in performance of students from the different-size schools. Several factors (variables) tend to make a generalization to a larger population less reliable than other areas of comparison in this study. For example, the larger schools tended also to be in the metropolitan areas; the

[9]William R. Lewis, doctoral dissertation (Norman, University of Oklahoma, 1972), 43.

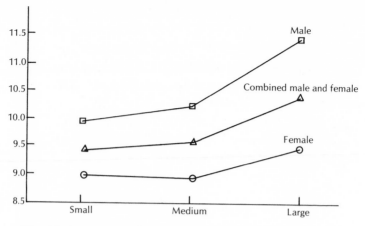

Fig. 16. Average total scores on all six tasks by school size

small schools were more likely to be in farm communities and smaller towns. This means that the extraschool environment was significantly different. This note of caution should be kept in mind in examining Figure 16.

There appears to be little difference in the over-all average scores of students in small schools and those of students in medium-sized schools. If compared on the basis of sex, boys do better in medium-sized schools than those in small schools, and the opposite is true for girls. Students from large schools perform much better than those in either medium or small schools. Again, the sex difference is evident, but size of school appears to influence males more than it does females.

The question concerning intellectual development as it is related to sex and school size is not fully answered in this research. We have only "opened the package." It is to be hoped that the answers to these questions will be pursued by other investigators so that curriculum developers, teachers, administrators, and legislators will have a better understanding of them to use in decision making.

When one examines the first-year college curriculum, it is evident that it contains primarily formal operational concepts. Most college freshmen are eighteen years of age, and yet the dropout rate during the freshman year is the highest in all college years. Why do students leave college during their first year? No doubt disinterest and social reasons explain part of that dropout rate, but many leave college because, they say, "It is too hard." What does a student who makes that remark mean? Is he saying that he is concrete-operational and that the work is formal-operational? Chapter 7 deals with our study of college freshmen and describes a specific curriculum program we used to test the hypothesis that operational stages at that educational level can be changed.

7. The College Student and Formal Operations

Joe W. McKinnon

The 1969 freshman class in all the United States colleges and universities was some 1.5 million strong and represented the nation's educational elite. By means of various testing procedures, students were sorted, sifted, and evaluated to determine whether student A was better able to do college-level work than student B. If, after appropriate analyses, the college admissions office had done a good job of selection, the professors had the very best minds available with which to work. Professors, however, complained that students did not seem to be able to understand the fundamental principles underlying the disciplines.

In the preceding chapters evidence has been cited to show that students at various grade levels have not yet achieved formal operational abilities, but surely by the time a student enters college he should be able to think clearly and logically. He should, at the very least, be able to handle ratio and proportion or fathom the complexities of a change of form of an object while it conserves its essential properties. He should be able to

110

suggest alternative solutions to problems in light of new information, and he should be able to separate the effect of a variable upon some system to determine whether or not the variable is relevant. These should at the very least comprise a reasonable set of expectations for the college professor.

The professor expects his students to be capable of independent thinking, to interact in situations demanding clear and rational thought and to combine that thought with expressive communicative techniques. He also expects the student to become conversant with subjects that are relatively unrelated to his chosen area of concentration. Saying, therefore, that college professors consider the college freshman capable of dealing with new and unusual situations in a competent manner and thinking rationally about them is not unreasonable. A college freshman should have enough background to be able to perform transformations upon newly acquired data and incorporate them into his mental framework. In other words, the college student should be capable of logical thought—to reason with abstract propositions that he will meet in his college courses.

Unfortunately, the college professor is often poorly informed about the true nature of his student's abilities. He assumes that the college student thinks logically. But has that student arrived at the formal operational stage of thought? If not, the professor will probably begin at a level of abstraction the student simply cannot understand.

The evidence available indicates that about 50 per cent of students entering college cannot cope with abstract propositions (this figure does not differ appreciably from college to college). These students cannot use the propositional logic referred to in Chapter 4. Supposing that college freshmen cannot use propositional logic, one would suspect that the student's college education would contribute to his acquisition of formal-operational thought. College students are generally not given the learning opportunities they need to develop logical thought with abstract propositions, because the college professor probably assumes that those mental abilities have already been developed. This assumption often leads the professor to create educational situations with which the student cannot cope and may contribute to the high attrition rates seen in today's institutions of higher education.

Formal Thought of College Freshmen

The question of formal operations among college freshmen has been of great concern to us for some time. Previous studies have indicated that most incoming students at one institution were unable to think logically.[1] Was this true of widely differing kinds of higher educational institutions having different educational purposes? The one institution tested was a liberal-arts college whose students compared very well nationally on conventional tests. If students in the state's four-year colleges or two-year junior colleges were tested, what would be found? To answer this question, seven representative institutions of higher education were selected, and a random sample of each institution's population was obtained. Freshman English classes were randomly sampled, since nearly all freshmen enroll in that course.

The first institution included in the research is a private university. Most of its students plan to continue their education beyond the four-year program. This university is above average in terms of the scores its students receive on the evaluation instruments of the American College Testing Program (ACT) and in comparison with similar institutions across the United States.[2] The second institution, a public university, is representative of universities in the United States. Its student body is above average for similar institutions in terms of ACT

---

[1] Joe W. McKinnon and John W. Renner, "Are Colleges Concerned with Intellectual Development?" *American Journal of Physics*, Vol. 39 (September, 1971), 1047–52.

[2] *American College Testing Program: College Student Profiles* (Iowa City, ACT Publications, 1966).

scores. The third institution is a small sectarian private college representing a fundamentalist group. Many of its students indicated in one way or another an interest in religious training. The fourth and fifth institutions are typical five-year state colleges that draw from a predominantly rural population. The fifth institution differs from the fourth only in that it draws from a Negro population and has a slightly higher percentage of large-city school students. The sixth institution is a two-year traditional junior college; many of its students come from a more prosperous agricultural area or from conservative, middle-class smaller cities. A prime function of this institution is to provide its students two years of undergraduate educational preparation before their entrance into one of the state universities. The seventh institution is a small, private, city-community college catering to students seeking a terminal, business-oriented education. Many of its students are from lower-middle-class backgrounds. These samples of students were tested with the following tasks described more fully in Chapter 4. The numbering of these tasks conforms to the numbering used in that chapter:

1. Conservation of solid amount
2. Conservation of weight
3. Conservation of volume using clay used in task 2
4. Conservation of volume using two identically shaped cylinders of different weights
6. Elimination of contradiction
8. Exclusion of irrelevant variables

Table 17 provides an analysis of performance by task and operational stage of the students of each school. The numbers shown in the columns represent the numbers of students who actually performed the given task at the particular stage. The right-hand column gives the percentage of students who performed at the highest possible level on the particular task. For tasks 6 and 8 the percentages shown in the parentheses are those of the students who performed at the formal-operational

Table 17. Analysis of Student Performance by School, Task, and Operational Stage

Institution	Sample size	Task	Operational Level					Per cent Achieving Highest Possible Level
			Concrete			Formal		
			I	IIA	IIB	IIIA	IIIB	
1	36	1		36				100
		2	2	0	34			94
		3	0	0	36			78
		4	7	0	0	29		81
		6	2	10	4	11	9	25(56)
		8	2	4	9	4	17	47(57)
2	25	1	1	24				96
		2	2	0	23			92
		3	0	0	25			76
		4	6	0	1	18		72
		6	2	8	6	2	7	28(36)
		8		7	6	4	8	32(48)
3	34	1	0	34				100
		2	14		20			59
		3	7		27			53
		4	6			28		82
		6	5	15	5	3	6	18(26)
		8	6	15	5	1	7	21(24)
4	19	1	0	19				100
		2	1	0	18			95
		3	1	0	18			63
		4	0	1	10	8		42
		6	0	8	4	2	5	26(37)
		8	0	6	2	4	7	37(58)
5	24	1	1	23				95
		2	2	0	22			92
		3	0	0	24			58
		4	0	8	4	12		50
		6	1	12	10	1		0(4)
		8	2	10	7	3	2	8(21)
6	39	1	0	39				100
		2	3	0	36			92
		3	7	0	32			54
		4	4	0	0	35		90
		6	7	13	3	6	10	26(41)
		8	4	8	8	8	11	28(49)
7	8	1	0	8				100
		2	0	0	8			100
		3	0	0	8			12
		4	5	0	0	3		38
		6	0	5	3	0		0(0)
		8	1	2	4	1		0(12)

($N = 185$)

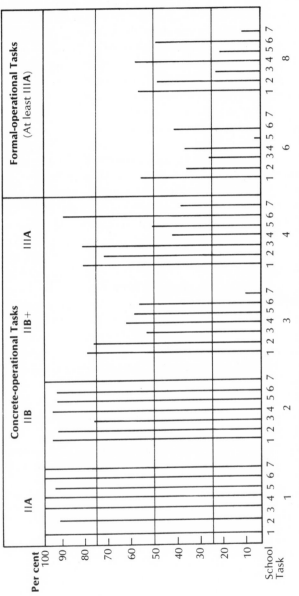

Fig. 17. Comparison of per cent success by institution on those tasks that define logical operations (1, 2, 3, 4, 6, and 8)

level, either III*A* or III*B*. For example, in the first institution 25 per cent (9 of 36) performed at the III*B* level on task 6 and 56 per cent (20 of 36) performed at the III*A* or III*B* level. The information from the percentage column of Table 17 is presented in graphic form in Figure 17; the percentage of values shown in parentheses was used for the last two tasks.

Since 185 students from the seven institutions were questioned on each of the three formal tasks (4, 6, and 8), 555 formal-operational responses were possible. By actual count 284 (51 per cent) concrete-operational responses were given. In 1969, 143 students were tested on these tasks, together with certain others.[3] Although a different method of scoring was used and the students tested were from one institution, *51 per cent of them operated at the concrete-operational level*. This result would suggest that the tasks, as outlined by Inhelder and Piaget,[4] do in fact yield valid measures of concrete and formal operations when given by persons who are familiar with their administration.

Table 18 answers the question how concrete- or formal-operational are the students from a particular institution? Column 2 compares student responses on the conservation of volume (task 4) by institution. (Goodrow and Bethon have shown that this task is not particularly sensitive to schooling.)[5] Column 3 provides a comparison of the percentages of students who scored more than eleven points and were thus considered to be operating at the formal-operational level, column 4 gives the average scores of students in the schools, and column 5 provides ACT score comparisons.

A comparison of ACT composite scores and scores on the Piagetian tasks has been reported by McKinnon and Renner.[6]

[3]Joe W. McKinnon, "The Influence of a College Inquiry-centered Course in Science on Student Entry into the Formal Operational Stage" doctoral dissertation (Norman, University of Oklahoma, 1970).

[4]Inhelder and Piaget, *The Growth of Logical Thinking.*

[5]Jacqueline Goodnow and Gloria Bethon, "Piaget's Tasks: The Effects of School and Intelligence," *Child Development*, Vol. 37, No. 3 (1966), 574–82.

Table 18. A Comparison of the Degree of Logical Operations Among Students of Different Institutions

Nature of Institution	Task 4 (Per cent Achieving IIIA)	Formal-Operational (Per cent Achieving More Than 11 Points)	Average Score	ACT Comparison Averages
1. 4-year private university	80	61	12.25	21.3
2. 6-year public university	76	52	11.48	22.4
3. 4-year private sectarian college	82	26	9.40	20.2
4. 5-year public teacher's college	42	46	11.70	18.3
5. 5-year public Negro university	50	12	9.70	12.0
6. 2-year public junior college	92	56	11.79	17.9
7. 2-year private community college	38	12	7.60	15.0

The comparison showed that students who had ACT scores of twenty-two (national average) or more also scored high on the Piagetian tasks; in other words, the correlation between ACT scores and Piagetian scores was high. When students scored less than twenty-two, however, the correlation was near zero. The data shown in Table 18 demonstrate that when ACT scores are in the neighborhood of twenty-two (institutions 1 and 2) Piagetian scores tend to also be high. The data from

[6]McKinnon and Renner, "Are Colleges Concerned with Intellectual Development?" *American Journal of Physics*, Vol. 39 (September, 1971), 1048.

institutions 3 through 7 show that, when the ACT scores are below twenty-two, the relationship between them and the Piagetian score is unstable. The data here seem to confirm, therefore, the McKinnon-Renner contention of the low relationship between the capacity for logical thought and the ACT score. Since approximately 50 per cent of entering college freshmen have ACT scores below twenty-two, large numbers of students are involved. This point, we believe, deserves further research to ascertain its exact meaning.

An Institution-designed Course to Promote Formal Thought: A Case Study

Introductory courses in science aimed at the first-year college student who will most likely not major in science differ in detail across the country but in general are similar in their approach in that they are designed to accommodate large numbers of students at minimal cost. The drawbacks to this approach have been recognized, and the literature abounds with suggestions for alleviating the situation. Very little concrete revision of such science courses, however, together with evaluations, has come out of these criticisms. One such revision was tested by McKinnon at a private university which was very much concerned with overcoming these problems.[7] This concern culminated in a call for the revision of the basic general-science education offering and led to the development of a course called "Forum for Scientific Inquiry." Basic to the course was the insistence that all the elements of inquiry—questioning, classifying, hypothesizing, verifying, restructuring, interpreting, and synthesizing—must be included. Other guidelines established by the faculty committee included the following:

1. The course would be team-taught by members from all areas of science. Although this did not necessarily mean that

[7]McKinnon, "The Influence of a College Inquiry-centered Course in Science on Student Entry into the Formal Operational Stage," 25.

College courses designed to promote formal thought must encourage social interaction.

the approach taken is inherently better than a single teacher's approach might be, it did mean that their expert advice upon a subject of their own choosing would be available to students.

2. "Forum for Scientific Inquiry" would not specify a particular set of facts of science as being necessary.

3. The lecture method would largely be abolished. More discussion, small-group seminars, and independent library study would take its place.

4. The laboratory approach would be more broadly interpreted to mean that those experiences necessary to provide the basic understanding of a particular problem that a student would be engaged in solving.

5. The text would become optional or discarded with a greater dependence upon articles and journals of interest.

Those planning the course hypothesized that, by following these guidelines, the objections and pitfalls by which such new efforts in curriculum revision had previously failed could be overcome and that a substantial increase in logical thought in students would result.

Structure of "Forum for Scientific Inquiry"

The new one-semester course "Forum for Scientific Inquiry" was designed in three major parts as shown in the diagram below:

6 weeks	2 weeks	6 weeks (2) (2) (2)

During the first six weeks of the semester, science students met in formal session for two one-hour periods a week, when one of the ten professors teaching the course presented a topic around which that week's work was built. The topics chosen for the first six week period included: (1) "The Nature of Science," (2) "The Nature of Mathematics," (3) "Scientific Concepts of Broad Applicability," (4) "Science as a Human Endeavor," (5) "Science as a Creative Enterprise," and (6) "Science and Responsibility."

The six topics were not mandatory and changed from semester to semester, depending upon the group of professors involved in the course, the topics were, however, mutually agreed upon by all involved before the semester began; by this procedure new faculty members could easily be integrated into the group. Following the one-hour presentation students met in small groups with one professor for the entire six weeks to discuss and research the topic of the week.

In the first semester the course was offered, six paperback books, selected by the coordinating group of professors, were used to supplement the material, but no test was given over any of the material. Students were asked to examine particular aspects of a problem, to find out what was known, and then to suggest how they might interpret those data to advance a solution or approach a better understanding of the problem. Twice a week the small groups met under the leadership of a fellow student, with the professor serving only to suggest alternatives; he did not present himself as an authority figure. The professors had varying degrees of success; however, all of them felt that the solutions or understandings of problems arose in the students' minds and were not those of the professors. During the coordinating faculty sessions held weekly, several professors qualitatively expressed an increasing confidence in the students' capacity to think more logically as compared with the students' initial efforts.

After the first six weeks all the students were involved in a two-week, small-group seminar (with a maximum of ten enrollees) offered by various professors in the College of Arts and Sciences. Although the topic was chosen by a professor, the student selected the seminar that was of most interest to him. No effort was made to direct the student's activities toward a particular seminar, even though he might be enrolled in a related course. He was free to choose from the full spectrum of seminar offerings of the College of Arts and Sciences.

The last six weeks of the course were broken into three sessions of two weeks each. For two of the three sessions the student attended a seminar of his own choice dealing with topics that the class as a whole had selected as being relevant to him. Each of the ten professors took a particular topic for the three sessions. By this means each student came into contact with three different professors as he selected from among the various topics available to him. The third session was a mathematics laboratory and was the only common experience of all the students in the course. Each student received a two-week introduction to the use of the computer in the mathematics laboratory. For four two-hour periods he was given practical rudiments of programming, shown how a program was written,

Group	Stage	Pretest		Posttest		Net gain		
		Females	*Males*	*Females*	*Males*	*Females*	*Males*	*Total*
Experi-mental	Formal	4	11	14	16	10	5	15
	Transitional	14	6	17	8	3	2	5
	Concrete	24	10	11	3	−13	−7	−20
Control	Formal	4	14	7	17	3	3	6
	Transitional	6	6	11	7	5	1	6
	Concrete	26	6	18	2	−8	−4	−12

Table 19. A Comparison of the Growth in Logical-Thought Processes of the Two Groups After the Course "Forum for Scientific Inquiry"

and then permitted to carry out the programming and verification of a simple series of calculations.

The student's concluding effort was to write a paper based on one of the first six-week topics, discussing the particular topic's value as applied to his own thinking. Grading in the course was based on a three-point system of honor's credit, credit, and no credit. Much of the effort by the student was self-generated, and, in general, this teaching technique was well received by him. A qualitative outcome of the course appeared to be a much higher level of extraclass discussion carried on elsewhere. Many students reported holding dormitory and luncheon discussions of great length.

The ten faculty members involved in the course concluded that the approaches taken were sound and resulted in greatly added interest and understanding by college students of the nature of science and the persons involved in scientific pursuits. Quantitative evaluation of the course was based on an increase in the students' capacity to think logically. The results of that investigation are shown in Tables 19 and 20.

Table 20. Pretest and Posttest Piagetian Mean for Experimental and Control Groups

Group	Experimental		Control	
	N	Piaget Score	N	Piaget Score
Pretest	69	10.77	62	10.81
Posttest	69	12.32	62	11.14

An Experiment with the Value of the "Forum for Scientific Inquiry"—Research Design and Testing of the Samples

During the fall semester 143 first-semester freshman college students were randomly separated into two groups at the time of enrollment. Slips numbered 1 through 300 were devised, stating whether or not each freshman student would enroll in the "Forum for Scientific Inquiry" during the first or the second semester. These slips were then evenly divided and arranged in a stack according to a table of random numbers. Each freshman student, upon receiving an enrollment packet, also received the next slip on top of the stack, and his name was written on it. The slip showed whether he would or would not enroll in the course "Forum for Scientific Inquiry," and was presented to his adviser during the enrollment period. The advisers had previously agreed to this procedure and with few exceptions enrolled the students according to the instructions given. Those students not enrolled in the first-semester science course became the control group.

Each of the 143 students was administered five Piagetian tasks at the beginning of the semester.[8] Six persons carried out the testing; all of them had had broad experience administering the Piagetian tasks to students of all ages and stages of logical thought. The tasks and means of scoring procedures were those discussed in Chapter 4. The tasks selected resulted in a possible 18-point total; a score of 0 to 10 was considered concrete-operational, a score of 11 to 13 was transitional (in the area between formal and concrete operations), and a score of 14 to 18 indicated formal operations. When the average pretest Piagetian scores for the two samples completing the posttest phase were compared, no significant difference was found between the two samples as indicated by an F ratio of less than 0.13. Composite ACT scores were 22.3 for the experimental group and 22.6 for the control group, while SAT verbal scores favored the control group by 10 points (469 to 459). The conclusion to be derived from these data is that no real difference existed between the two samples before the educational experiences provided by the experimental course, "Forum for Scientific Inquiry." Approximately 50 per cent of the sample

[8]The tasks selected to be used were conservation of volume using clay, reciprocal implication, elimination of contradictions, separation of variables, and exclusion; these tasks are described in Chapter 4.

group was enrolled in the experimental course in addition to other freshman courses, and the remainder selected courses from the usual freshman offerings. We assume, therefore, that any gains in formal-operational ability can be attributed to the experiences provided in the "Forum for Scientific Inquiry," because there is no reason for us to believe that any combination of courses is superior to another.

At the conclusion of the semester the same tasks were again administered, and 131 students completed the posttest phase. To ensure a neutral attitude by the task administrators, the students tested were not identified by control or experimental grouping. During the experimental treatment no specific mention was made of any of the principles involved in the various tasks. The major concern was whether concrete-operational students who participated in the experimental, inquiry-oriented course in science would exhibit greater growth in their capacity to think logically than did a similar group who did not participate. The null hypothesis arising from this question was evaluated by comparing the pretest and posttest results obtained from the experimental and control groups on the five Piagetian tasks. The data shown in Table 19 provide a comparison of the growth in the logical-thought processes of the two groups after the experimental group was exposed to the newly developed course.

The data in Table 19 show a net gain for the experimental group that resulted in fifteen students moving into the formal stage of thought, compared with six for the control group. The gain from the concrete to transitional stages was, respectively, five and seven, with the experimental group showing a net movement of twenty out of this category, compared with twelve for the control group, a net gain of more than 50 per cent for the group exposed to the influence of the inquiry course. Another comparison in terms of the mean Piagetian scores for the two groups is shown in Table 20.

Research described earlier in this chapter gives evidence that many students at various institutions of higher learning do not think abstractly. Through an experience like that provided in the "Forum for Scientific Inquiry," however, logical-thought processes of college freshmen can be enhanced. What steps does this research suggest should be taken?

Implications for Revising College Courses

The problems of students enrolling in introductory college courses are legion. Professors find themselves dealing with concepts that should be relatively obvious to what they believe represent the things that thinking college students can handle. All too often, however, this is not the case. Apparently the college freshman does not come to college prepared to carry out extensions of prior concrete thinking; that is, he is not yet capable of the abstract formulation of concepts without additional concrete experiences or without many added opportunities for forming abstract concepts through actual manipulation of materials and variables.

Elkind points to the three factors vital to education when viewed from the Piagetian framework.[9] At the forefront of Piaget's view of the child's developing reasoning abilities is the necessity for adequately structured experiences. This implies adequate, appropriate communication. If this view is accepted, together with the evidence presented here, the college must conclude that most college freshmen are not prepared to carry on the intellectual manipulations most freshman courses normally expect of them. If changes in course structure are made to accommodate to the concreteness of the students' thinking, growth in reasoning abilities can be enhanced. The study just described demonstrates that actual involvement of the student enhances his development of formal-operational thought.

The second major point brought out by Elkind is that the average student comes to college having a certain world view, whether or not correct. By providing opportunities to carry out

[9]David Elkind, *Children and Adolescents: Interpretive Essays on Jean Piaget* (New York, Oxford University Press, 1970), 84–85.

To promote formal thought, college courses must provide "hands-on" experiences with the materials of the discipline.

the manipulative experiences necessary to test his presumptions—that is, to hypothesize about the given concept—the student can adequately confirm his view or be forced to revise this view because of the contradictions that he must reconcile. Again, this approach was extensively used in the science program just described. The act of hypothesis formation followed by test is at the very heart of enhancement of logical thought, and, when these opportunities are given to students in abundance, they extend to other areas as well. In other words, hypothesis formation, the search for manipulative variables, and mental manipulation of these variables become a vital part of the cognitive structure.

Elkind's third point—that the zest for knowledge is present in children and must not be destroyed through rigid curricula—is more than adequately illustrated by the evidence presented here. College freshmen, wherever located, are not prepared to carry out mental manipulation of variables; therefore, they are not prepared to conceptualize as we would have them do in our college-level courses of today. The rigidity of most present-day college courses does little to create a zest for learning. If we value logical thinking, then changes must be toward courses that allow the, "Oh, now I see," experience—effective exploratory experience that leads to insight into phenomena. Only in this way can we fulfill our obligations to the students.

Various implications have been made about the underlying social structure that leads students to choose certain colleges and universities. Some schools, such as smaller, private, sectarian colleges, tend to enroll a disproportionate number of freshmen who do not think logically for reasons that probably do not relate to academic qualifications. The composite score average for the freshmen of institution 3 (Table 17) was only slightly below the best average scores reported, and yet the students ranked at the lowest level in ability to think logically. This suggests that other factors are operating. For example, an exceptionally authoritative home influence might lead the student to select a school that is of the same kind, even though the student's ACT score might permit him to attend other schools.

The Negro institution is selected by students for reasons that are more closely related to societal factors than to factors based on the quality of the education they might receive there. At the same time such a school serves a valid purpose for a significant segment of our population that some criterion of measurement, such as the average ACT score reported for its freshman students, tends to mask. The validity of this educational purpose would be further increased if its faculty were more aware of the stage of logical-thought development of their students and designed educational experiences that enhanced logical thinking.

Since students at most institutions are admitted on a basis that does not adequately separate those who are logical thinkers from those who are not, some alteration of the basic higher-education selection structure seems necessary. In turn, the implication for revision of the kinds of experiences that students have in *all* our higher educational institutions is mandatory.

If one examines the models upon which our four-year institutions are based, far too much similarity between today and the last century is evident; few, if any, innovative changes have been made. The assumption has been that certain levels of achievement were self-evident by reason of the student's high school diploma. From this the professor could reasonably expect certain levels of performance from his students. He could assume, among other things, the ability to think logically and proceeded to design his courses accordingly. The data presented in this chapter and in Chapter 6 demonstrate that this assumption is not valid.

For those institutions whose doors must be open to all who would attend, or who draw from certain segments of our society, extensive revision of aims and goals is vital. The Negro university must create experiences leading to logical thought. Universities such as this are vital as a means of upgrading the skills of a significant segment of our Negro population regardless of the beginning point of that higher education. Those persons charged with the curricular structure of the institution, however, must be cognizant of the underlying difficulty and bring about the changes called for. The same general statements could be made for the other higher-education institutions in our sample.

8. A Statistical Analysis of Piaget's Tasks

Anton E. Lawson

The question whether intellectual development occurs in stages or as a gradual continuum has long been pondered by psychologists and educators. Although that question is not answered by the statistical analyses reported here, there is support for Piaget's constructs of concrete-operational and formal-operational modes of thinking.

Through the use of the statistical technique of principal-components analysis the Piagetian task scores of the study of seventh- through twelfth-grade secondary school students reported in Chapter 6, the study of college freshmen in Chapter 7, and the study of eighth- and ninth-grade science students reported in Chapter 5 have been analyzed.

The Technique

Before the comments on results of these analyses, a brief introduction to the technique of principal-components analysis is in order. Basically, principal-components analysis is a multivariate technique, which is often considered a first-stage solution in factor analysis. The technique can be used to determine factorial validity of psychological tests, and that is one way in which it is used here. Generally, the technique attempts to reduce mathematically a set of many measures to a smaller number of factors by extracting weighted sums of those measures which account for a maximum amount of the variance of the total set. For example, if one tests schoolteachers with twenty-five separate tests to measure teacher effectiveness, one obtains twenty-five separate scores. By analysis of this set of twenty-five scores with principal components, the number of scores that contribute to most of the variance between good and bad teaching can be accounted for by perhaps only four or five of the measures. Instead of using twenty-five separate tests to determine teacher effectiveness, one needs now to use only four or five. Principal-components analysis, therefore, effects a parsimony of description.

To use the technique to validate psychological tests such as the Piagetian tasks, the procedure is relatively simple. A set of six formal operational Piagetian tasks, for instance, should be reduced to only one factor through the use of principal components. Since the tasks presumably measure only one thing, only one principal component should be extracted, and all six tasks should correlate highly or load heavily on the component. This result would validate the tasks in that they would indeed seem all to be measuring the same thing, namely, formal-operational thought. If the technique extracts more than one principal component, or root, then one would conclude that the tasks measure more than one thing. A result such as this would invalidate the tasks.

If a series of both concrete and formal tasks is analyzed, it would be possible to determine the number of psychological factors (components) that underlay success on these tasks. It is necessary to keep in mind that it remains the responsibility of the investigator to determine the "psychological meaningfulness" of the factors. Using this procedure, we have analyzed the data collected on the performances on Piagetian tasks and attempted to gain a further insight into the validity of the tasks and, in this case, the meaningfulness of viewing development as occurring in concrete and formal stages.

The Results

The first sample analyzed was that of 514 seventh- to twelfth-grade students from Oklahoma public schools. See Chapter 6 for a discussion of the sampling techniques used. Note that the sample size was 588. The number of subjects used here is fewer since 74 of the subjects lacked a complete set of the six Piagetian scores. The six Piagetian tasks administered were the conservation of solid amount, conservation of weight, conservation of volume using clay, conservation of volume using cylinders, elimination of contradiction, and exclusion. The data were analyzed twice by principal-components analysis with the use of the program FACTOR.[1] First, all components, or roots, were extracted, and, second, the program extracted only those components corresponding to *eigenvalues*[2] of the correlation matrix that were greater than unity. The procedure of extracting components with roots greater than one is perhaps, at present, the most widely used procedure. The rule was first proposed by Kaiser in 1960.[3] Table 21 shows the results after a variance-maximizing rotation of the axes was carried out and only roots with values greater than one were extracted. Only two principal components were extracted, and 55.2 per

[1]Donald J. Veldman, *Fortran Programing for the Behavioral Sciences* (New York, Holt, Rinehart and Winston, 1967), 219–36.

[2]The term *eigenvalue* is essentially synonymous with the terms *root, latent root,* or *characteristic root* commonly used in a branch of matrix algebra. For a mathematical treatment of these terms see Maurice M. Tatsuoka, *Multivariate Analysis: Techniques for Educational and Psychological Research* (New York, John Wiley and Sons, 1971), 125–43 (hereafter cited as *Multivariate Analysis*).

[3]H. F. Kaiser, "The Application of Electronic Computers to Factor Analysis," *Educational and Psychological Measurement*, Vol. 20 (1960), 141–51.

(N=514)

Task	First Component Loading, 31.35 Per Cent of Variance	Second Component Loading, 23.84 Per Cent of Variance	Per Cent Communality
Conservation of solid amount	−0.0098	0.7758	60.2019
Conservation of weight	0.0952	0.7895	63.2426
Conservation of volume using clay	0.4544	0.4402	40.0309
Conservation of volume using cylinders	0.7572	0.0883	58.1118
Elimination of contradictions	0.7479	0.0466	56.1547
Exclusion	0.7299	0.0413	53.4488

Table 21. Varimax Rotation Analysis, Seventh- to Twelfth-Grade Students in Oklahoma Public Schools

cent of the variance of the sample scores was accounted for by these two components. That percentage represents a relatively large or respectable portion of the variance.[4]

In that the six tasks were designed to measure only two kinds of thinking patterns (concrete- and formal-operational thought), this result was predicted by the model. A graphic presentation of these data is shown in Figure 18.

All six tasks, with the exception of task 3, load well or correlate highly with one of the two principal components. Since both task 1, conservation of solid amount, and task 2, conservation of weight, correlate highly (0.77 and 0.78 respectively) with the second principal component, we concluded that the second component, or factor, represented concrete-operational thinking. Piaget contends that both these tasks measure concrete-operational thought, and thus this result was also as predicted.

Task 4 through 6, conservation of volume using cylinders, elimination of contradictions, and exclusion, were designed to measure formal-operational thinking. Note that all three tasks correlated highly (0.75, 0.74, and 0.72 respectively) with the first principal component. In light of this result it seemed clear that the first principal component represented formal-operational thought. This again was as expected in terms of Piagetian theory and, in essence, factorially validates these three tasks.

It should be mentioned that, although the conservation-of-volume task using cylinders is labeled a conservation problem, it is unlike the concrete-operational-conservation tasks on two points. First, it involves the abstract concept of water displacement. Second, it requires the subject to eliminate a contradiction. He must be able to ignore what his senses tell him in terms of the unequal weights of the objects and instead focus his attention on the equal volumes to complete the task successfully. Both of these points make the task formal.

[4]For discussion of statistical techniques used to determine significant components and variances see Tatsuoka, *Multivariate Analysis*, 146–47.

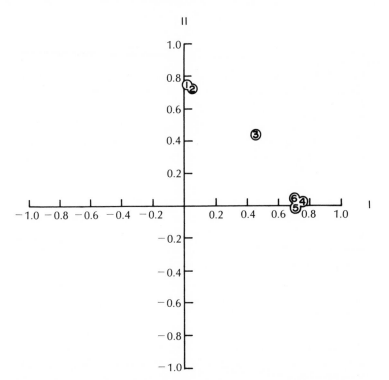

Fig. 18. Factor structure of Piagetian tasks, Oklahoma seventh- to twelfth-grade students (**N**=514). Task (1) conservation of solid amount; (2) conservation of weight; (3) conservation of volume using clay; (4) conservation of volume using cylinders; (5) elimination of contradiction; (6) exclusion of variables

Of particular interest is the task on conservation of volume using clay. Note that this task correlates moderately with both principal components (0.45 and 0.44). At first consideration this seems to contradict Piaget's contention that the task measures formal-operational thought. However, it should be noted that Piaget, in discussing the task himself, has suggested that the conservation of volume may incorporate certain concrete aspects. In referring to the concept of conservation of volume, Piaget states:

That construction belongs to stage IV (Formal Operational Thought), but it may be that there is also a conservation of volume in a simpler form, one which does not entail the calculation of volume together with the elaboration of metrical relations between the volume under consideration and the surfaces by which it is bounded. Because that notion would be merely qualitative, it might well appear at level IIIA (late concrete operational thought), together with the conservation of length, and area.

Thus, although Piaget contends that conservation of volume using clay represents formal-operational thought, he acknowledges the possibility that certain aspects of the task require only concrete thought processes, and, therefore, can be successfully solved on occasion by concrete-operational thinking. That is precisely what these data indicated, with the moderate correlations of 0.45 and 0.44 of this task with the first and the second principal components.

In concluding the analysis of this particular sample, it can be said that on all points the results are as Piagetian theory predicts: (1) only two components, concrete- and formal-operational thought, are measured by the six tasks; (2) the tasks conservation of solid amount and conservation of weight measure essentially one factor; (3) the tasks conservation of volume using cylinders, elimination of contradiction, and exclusion also essentially measure one factor; (4) the conservation of volume using clay, somewhat surprisingly, indicated a certain amount of both formal and concrete thinking, a result that was also anticipated by Piaget.

While these results do not definitely indicate distinct stages in intellectual growth, they suggest that Piaget's tasks measure what they are supposed to measure and that the constructs of formal-operational thought and concrete-operational thought seem viable.

College Freshmen

The study involving first-year college students reported in Chapter 7 provided additional data that were used to analyze further the effectiveness of Piagetian tasks. In that study five tasks were used to assess levels of intellectual development of 142 students. The tasks were the conservation of volume using clay, reciprocal implications, elimination of contradiction, separation of variables, and exclusion. The two tasks reciprocal implications and separation of variables were not analyzed in the sample of high school students in seventh through twelfth grade. We, therefore, were given the opportunity to validate these additional tasks. The results of the analysis are shown in Table 22. By using varimax rotation and by extracting roots with values greater than one, only one root was extracted, which accounted for 48.38 per cent of the variance. The four formal operational tasks loaded heavily on this component (0.76, 0.80, 0.80, and 0.68, respectively). The conservation-of-volume task using clay loaded at only 0.25 on this component, an expected result, since this component represents formal-operational thought while the task probably measures some concrete thinking, as stated by Piaget.

Table 22. Varimax Rotation Analysis, College Freshmen
($N = 142$)

Task	*First Component Loading 48.3 Per Cent of Variance*	*Per Cent communality*
Conservation of volume using clay	0.2547	6.4895
Reciprocal implication	0.7681	59.0014
Elimination of contradiction	0.8053	64.8517
Separation of variables	0.8068	65.0972
Exclusion	0.6818	46.4805

Junior High School Science Students

One additional sample of data has been analyzed—that reported in Chapter 5—which was composed of experiments with eighth- and ninth-grade science students. In that research 209 subjects were administered six Piagetian tasks: conservation of solid amount, conservation of volume using cylinders, reciprocal implications, elimination of contradiction, separation of variables, and exclusion. The results of the principal-components analysis are shown in Table 23.

Table 23. Varimax Rotation Analysis, Eighth- and Ninth-Grade Science Students

$(N = 209)$

Task	First Component Loading 39.77 Per Cent of Variance	Per Cent communality
Conservation of solid amount	0.5092	25.9278
Conservation of volume using cylinders	0.4828	23.3073
Reciprocal implications	0.6626	43.8993
Elimination of contradiction	0.6965	48.5075
Separation of variables	0.7668	58.7977
Exclusion	0.6183	38.2254

When roots with values greater than one were extracted, only one principal component was isolated. This component accounted for 39.77 per cent of the variance, a figure not as high as expected. Four of the formal tasks, reciprocal implications, elimination of contradictions, separation of variables, and exclusion, loaded substantially on this component (0.66, 0.69, 0.76, and 0.61, respectively).

Unexpectedly, the conservation of solid amount loaded at 0.50 with this component. Since this was a concrete-operational task, and we assumed that this component represented formal-operational thought, this correlation seems high. Notice, however, that, while it loaded at 0.50, only 25.9 per cent of the communality, or common-factor, variance was accounted for by this task, indicating that, although the task loaded moderately on this component, a substantial portion of the variance could have been accounted for by a second component if it had been extracted.

A further unexpected result was that the conservation of volume using cylinders task loaded at only 0.48 on this component. We have no explanation for this result, which is inconsistent with those reported above.

Conclusions

These results, we believe, offer significant support for Piaget's constructs of concrete- and formal-operational thinking and, therefore, to his theory of stages of intellectual development. The question whether persons pass from one mode of thinking to another in distinct steps or in a slow, gradual progression has not been investigated. What appears clear from these results are two separate and distinct forms of thought processes used by students from seventh grade through first-year college in responding to the various Piagetian tasks administered.

How the research relates to the role of today's schools and the promotion of thought from one level to the next is the question discussed in Chapter 9.

9. A Study of the Piagetian Model as Directly Applied to Science Subject Matter

Anton E. Lawson

New secondary school science programs have been developed in recent years that not only update the content of science teaching but emphasize the laboratory as a means to student inquiry.[1] These new programs further attempt to reflect accurately the structure of the particular discipline, be it chemistry, physics, or biology. For example, the Biological Science Curriculum Study has three versions of inquiry-oriented biology textbooks available for school use. Each textbook emphasizes one selected area in biology—ecology, cell biology, or molecular biology. Although each text emphasizes different areas of biology, nine basic unifying themes pervade each one:

1. Change of living things through time: evolution
2. Diversity of type and unity of pattern in living things

[1]For reviews of these programs see P. Dehart Hurd, *New Directions in Teaching Secondary School Science* (Chicago, Rand McNally and Co., 1969); and P. Dehart Hurd, *New Curriculum Perspectives for Junior High School Science* (Belmont, Calif., Wadsworth Co., 1970).

3. The genetic continuity of life
4. The complementarity of organism and environment
5. The biological roots of behavior
6. The complementarity of structure and function
7. Regulation and homeostasis preservation of life in the face of change.
8. The history of biological conceptions
9. Science as inquiry[2]

Project Physics, which originated at Harvard University in 1962, includes in its program a textbook, student guides for each unit, a laboratory guide, laboratory equipment, audiovisual material, teacher's guides, and an evaluation program. The units of the text reflect the program's adherence to the fundamental concepts of the discipline. The units are (1) "Concepts in Motion," (2) "Motion in the Heavens," (3) "Energy," (4) "Waves and Fields," (5) "Models of the Atom," and (6) "The Nucleus."[3]

In the field of chemistry new programs are also in evidence. One such program is the CHEM Study Program, which evolved out of a committee established in 1959 by the American Chemical Society. CHEM Study materials include a text, a laboratory manual, teacher's guides, instruction pamphlets, achievement tests, related monographs, and films.[4] The content and structure of the textbook also clearly demonstrate an adherence to the major concepts and principles of the discipline.

During the time these new science programs were being constructed, the works of Piaget were beginning to receive greater and greater attention. Piaget's stages of intellectual development, as outlined earlier, provide a possible tool for the evaluation of school curricula in terms of the intellectual ability of the students. First, Piaget has provided tests for the assessment of levels of thinking. Second, he has detailed the kinds of understanding and thought processes available to individuals at each level. School curricula can now be analyzed in terms of

[2]Hurd, *New Directions in Teaching Secondary School Science*, 154.
[3]*Ibid.*, 193–96.
[4]*Ibid.*, 177–78.

the concrete or formal nature of the major concepts taught to determine whether students for whom those curricula were designed are capable of achieving the desired understanding.

Piaget's theory clearly predicts that concrete operational students will not be able to develop understanding of abstract concepts—that is, concepts that require the building of theories and departures from concrete reality. It is also implied that formal-operational students will be able to develop understanding of both concrete and abstract concepts.

According to the Piagetian model, formal thought begins to develop at age eleven or twelve and reaches an equilibrium state at around age fifteen or sixteen. If this is true, then the formal nature of the new secondary school science programs is probably appropriate in that most students enrolled in these classes will be formal thinkers. A good deal of recent research, however, indicates that, to the contrary, perhaps 40 to 75 per cent of secondary school students have failed to reach the level of formal thought.

If Piagetian theory is correct and if indeed a large number of secondary school students are concrete-operational, then the major portion of today's science curricula is beyond the student's level of understanding and, therefore, inappropriate. The conclusion Kohlberg and Gilligan came to when they stated that "clearly these new curricula assumed formal operational thought rather than attempting to develop it"[5] deserves a careful analysis.

Problem Statement

This analysis of secondary school science subject matter in relation to the Piagetian model has as its primary objective the assessment of understanding of concrete and formal operational

---

[5]Kohlberg and Gilligan, "The Adolescent as Philosopher: The Discovery of the Self in a Postconventional World" *Daedalus*, Vol. 100, No. 4 (Fall, 1971), 1082.

concepts by concrete and formal operational students in secondary school biology, chemistry, and physics classes.

To accomplish this objective, the percentages of concrete- and formal-operational students in selected biology, chemistry, and physics classes were determined, and individual subjects were identified as concrete- or formal-operational thinkers. Six Piagetian-styled tasks were used to assess levels of thinking. The major concepts taught during the year in each science class were classified as concrete- or formal-operational, and written tests involving those concepts were constructed and administered.

This study, then, sought answers to the following questions: What are the levels of intellectual development of selected students in biology, chemistry, and physics classes as determined by Piagetian tasks? What are the major concrete- and formal-operational concepts taught in those classes? What are the relationships between students' scores on the Piagetian tasks and written test scores on concrete- and formal-operational concepts; in other words, are concrete-operational students able to understand only concrete concepts while formal operational students are able to understand both concrete- and formal operational concepts?

Definitions

Before the investigation was undertaken, precise definitions of the terms *concrete-operational concept, formal-operational concept,* and *understanding* were needed. No previous attempt at a classification of concepts into concrete or formal categories was uncovered in a literature search undertaken before the construction of these definitions. The definitions below are provided to allow a concept, once isolated, to be categorized as concrete- or formal-operational, requiring either concrete- or formal-operational thinking to develop "understanding" of the concept.

Concrete-operational concepts. Concrete-operational concepts are concepts whose meaning can be developed from firsthand experience with objects or events. These concepts may arise through intuition in which the entire meaning of the concept is given through the senses, such as the color "blue." Concrete concepts may also arise by postulation; however, if so, part of the meaning of the concept must be sensed or immediately apprehended. Examples are common objects, such as tables, chairs, and other persons.

Formal-operational concepts. Formal-operational concepts are concepts whose meanings are derived through position within a postulatory-deductive system. Meaning is given to these concepts not through senses but through imagination or through their logical relationships within the system. To comprehend fully the meaning of a formal concept, one must be able to operate formally or logically in a hypothetico-deductive manner, since a formal concept is one whose meaning, in whole or in part, is designated by postulates of the deductive theory in which it occurs. In other words, the concept's meaning is developed by virtue of the properties or relationships assigned to it by the postulate or set of postulates within which it is a member term.

Some formal concepts can be imagined with concrete models. The solid-particle model of atoms is an example of this kind of concept. The light model that borrows the pattern of waves on water is another example. Note that since concepts such as these can be modeled with the use of concrete objects, events, or symbols, concrete-operational individuals can develop the ability to verbalize about such things. However, they are denied a full comprehension of the concepts until the development of formal operations that allow construction of the postulatory-deductive system within which the concept derives its full meaning.

In evaluating comprehension of such concepts, it is imperative to avoid an evaluation based solely upon comprehension of concrete models. Such evaluation fails to test for understanding of a concept's implications.

Understanding. The classification scheme developed in *Taxonomy of Educational Objectives: The Classification of Educational Goals* (edited by Benjamin S. Bloom) was used to categorize examination questions to assess concept understanding. That scheme classifies educational goals into six levels: (1) knowledge, (2) comprehension, (3) application, (4) analysis, (5) synthesis, and (6) evaluation. Since level 1 questions require only recall, and levels 4 through 6 test for mental operations other than concept understanding, it was decided that questions developed here must be constructed with the use of levels 2 and 3 only.

Understanding, then, is operationally defined as the ability to select the correct, or best, response from among those given on multiple-choice questions involving items classified on the comprehension or application level of the above-mentioned taxonomy.

Procedures

Overview. Subjects for this study were selected from Norman High School, Norman, Oklahoma, a school with more than two thousand students, which offers classes in biology, chemistry, and physics. The students were taught in their science courses by the regular classroom teacher. During the last month of instruction in the 1972–73 academic year, the investigator administered six Piagetian tasks to subjects representatively sampled from each discipline.

Sample sizes were determined to comply with the statistical techniques used. (Although no strict rules exist, when multiple-correlation coefficients are calculated, approximately ten subjects are suggested for each independent variable.) In this study five formal operational Piagetian tasks were used; therefore, fifty-one subjects were representatively selected from biology classes, and fifty subjects were similarly selected from chemistry classes. From the only physics class all thirty-three subjects were selected. The subjects' responses on the Piagetian tasks were scored as preoperational (I), concrete-operational (IIA or IIB), or formal operational (IIIA or IIIB). Subject-matter tests were then administered to the subjects in their respective disciplines. These tests basically consisted of two parts: (1) evaluation of understanding of concrete-operational concepts and (2) evaluation of understanding of formal-operational concepts. Numerical scores were obtained for each subject on both parts of the test. Multiple-correlation coefficients were obtained and tested for significance by use of F tests.[6]

The data were further analyzed by use of stepwise semipartial regression techniques to determine which Piagetian task best predicted the subject's success on concrete- and formal-operational concepts.[7] Principal-components analysis was also used to determine the number of cognitive parameters underlying success on the six Piagetian tasks.[8]

Instruments

Six tasks patterned after Piaget and Inhelder were administered to each subject to determine intellectual development: one concrete-operational task, conservation of weight, and five formal-operational tasks. The tasks used were: (1) conservation of weight,[9] (2) conservation of volume,[10] (3) separation of variables,[11] (4) equilibrium in the balance,[12] (5) ratio,[13] and (6) the

[6]Tatsuoka, *Multivariate Analysis*, 26–38.

[7]Richard B. Darlington, "Multiple Regression in Psychological Research and Practice," *Psychological Bulletin*, Vol. 69 (1968), 178.

[8]Tatsuoka, *Multivariate Analysis*, 48.

[9]Renner and Stafford, *Teaching Science in the Secondary School*, 89–90.

[10]*The Developmental Theory of Piaget: Conservation* (film).

[11]Inhelder and Piaget, *The Growth of Logical Thinking*, 46–66.

[12]*Ibid.*, 164–81.

[13]Robert Karplus, Elizabeth F. Karplus, and Warren Wollman, "Intellectual Development Beyond Elementary School IV: Ratio, the Influence of Cognitive Style," unpublished manuscript, (Berkeley, University of California, 1973) (hereafter cited as "Ratio").

islands puzzle.[14] Subjects were scored separately on each task. Numerical scores were awarded on a one-to-five scale as follows:

1. I, Preoperational
2. II*A*, Transition to concrete-operational
3. II*B*, Concrete-operational
4. III*A*, Transition to formal-operational
5. III*B*, Formal-operational

Description of the Piagetian Tasks

Conservation of weight and conservation of volume. These tasks were administered and evaluated in the same manner as described earlier in this book.

Separation of variables. The subject was shown the apparatus, which consisted of six flexible metal rods of varying length, diameter, shape, and material. The rods were attached to a stationary block of wood with adjustable clamps. Weights of one hundred and two hundred grams were placed on the ends to demonstrate the flexible nature of the rods. The subject was also shown how to adjust the length of the rods by using the adjustable clamps. The subject was then asked to experiment with the apparatus until he could determine which of the rods bent the most and which bent the least.

After the experiment the subject was asked to explain why some rods bent more than others and to name the factors that determined how much the rods would bend. Following the naming of the factors, the subject was asked to prove the role of each of the factors mentioned. The subject who simply classified the rods that bent the most and/or least into thicker, thinner, longer, shorter, square, or round was classified as II*A*. The subject who classified but compared two rods with logical multiplication was categorized as II*B*. Logical multiplication

[14]Robert Karplus and Elizabeth F. Karplus, "Intellectual Development Beyond Elementary School I: Deductive Logic," *School Science and Mathematics*, May, 1970, pp. 398–99.

can be thought of as (thicker) × (longer) = (thinner) × (shorter); such a subject used compensation to explain what he saw. The distinguishing factor of a student in either class III*A* or class III*B* was his ability to demonstrate proof by utilizing the "all-things-being-equal" concept.

The subject who demonstrated that he could prove that one rod would not bend as much as another by holding, say, material, length, and weight (or any combination) constant and experimenting with the diameter was classified as III*A*. This subject would try to hold other variables constant and manipulate still others but fail in some cases.

The subject who identified all the variables (weight, length, material, shape, and diameter) and systematically set about holding all but one constant and testing that one until all were tested was classified as III*B* and was completely formal-operational.

Equilibrium in the balance. The subject was shown the apparatus, which consisted of a balance arm with thirty holes drilled in one-inch intervals along its length. Weights of ten units, five units, and two units, which could be hung in the holes, were also pointed out. The interviewer hung one ten-unit weight seven units of length from the fulcrum and asked the subject to hang another ten-unit weight on the opposite arm to achieve a balance.

Following completion of this experiment the subject was given two five-unit weights to replace one of the ten-unit weights and asked to place them on the arm to achieve a balance. While the subject determined the proper location for the five-unit weights, the interviewer held the arms of the balance parallel to the table surface. After the subject hung the weights, the interviewer released the arm to determine whether a balance had been achieved.

Next the subject removed his weights, was given one five-unit weight, and was asked to hang it to balance again the ten-unit weight. Again the examiner held the end of the balance arm. After the subject had selected the location, he was asked to explain his selection. Correct position selection *and* expla-

Mr. Short

Fig. 19. Mr. Short

nation placed the subject in category III*A*. Following the explanation the examiner released the balance arm again to see whether balance had been achieved. If the subject reasoned that the five-unit weight was five less than the ten-unit weight and therefore must be placed five units farther out, he used the *difference* between ten and five for his comparison, not the *ratio* of ten and five. This response was concrete and was categorized as II*B*. No systematic explanation or a response that indicated that the subject did not understand the law "heavier = nearer," placed the subject in category II*A*.

In a final task to differentiate III*A* and III*B* responses, the subject was given a seven-unit weight and asked to make it balance a ten-unit weight placed seven units from the center. Correct prediction and explanation of this more difficult proportion problem placed the subject in category III*B*.

Ratio. This task was administered to groups of subjects. Responses were written rather than oral. The subjects were given answer pages as shown in Figure 19 and a chain of number-1 Gem paper clips containing eight clips. The subjects were then told that there was a figure called Mr. Tall, similar to the Mr. Short on their papers but larger, in the experimenter's office. The experimenter explained: "I measured Mr. Short's height with large buttons, one on top of the other, starting with the floor between Mr. Short's feet and going to the top of his head." Four buttons reached to the top of his head. (At this point, the experimenter wrote "Mr. Short: 4 buttons" on the board.) "Then I measured Mr. Tall with the same buttons and found that he was six buttons high." ("Mr. Tall: 6 buttons" was written on the board.)

"Now," the experimenter said, "you do three things. First, you measure Mr. Short using your small paper clips. Then you predict the height of Mr. Tall if you could measure him with the paper clips. Then please explain how you figured out your prediction. Explain as best you can how you figured out the number of paper clips in your prediction."

Subjects with questions or requests for more information were referred to the data on the chalkboard and were encouraged to use their own ideas for answering the questions. The experimenter briefly scanned the papers when they were turned in and asked individuals with incomplete explanations to clarify their reasoning.

Subject responses were categorized by use of the procedures outlined by Karplus, Karplus, and Wollman.[15] Categories IC and S were considered equivalent to category II*A*. Categories A and AS were labeled II*B*, while categories PC and AP were considered III*A* responses. Subcategory R was equivalent to III*B* responses.

Islands puzzle. This task was administered to groups of subjects. Responses were written rather than oral. Each subject was given a written copy of the puzzle. The examiner explained that it was a puzzle to determine the various kinds of problem-solving methods used by persons of their age. The diagram of the islands was pointed out, and the introduction was presented. The first two clues and the first question were also read to the subjects. They were asked to respond with one of the three choices and explain their choice. The islands are shown in Figure 20, followed by the problem format.

[15]Karplus, Karplus, and Wollman, "Ratio," 2–3. The acronyms represent the following: IC, intuitive computation; S, scaling; A, addition; AS, addition and scaling; PC, proportion concrete; AP, addition and proportion; R, application of ratio.

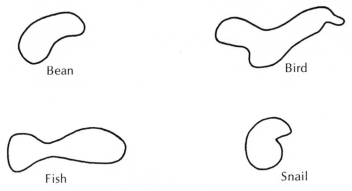

Fig. 20. Islands puzzle

Introduction: The puzzle is about four islands in the ocean. People have been traveling among these islands by boat for many years, but recently an airline started in business. Listen carefully to the clues I give you about possible plane trips. The trips may be direct or they may include stops on one of the islands. When I say a trip is possible, it can be made in both directions between the islands.

This is a map with the four islands, called Bean Island, Bird Island, Fish Island, and Snail Island. You may make notes or marks on your map to help you remember the clues. Raise your hand if you have questions about the clues.

First clue: People can go by plane between Bean and Fish Islands.

Second clue: People cannot go by plane between Bird and Snail Islands.

Use these two clues to answer Question 1.

Question 1: Can people go by plane between Bean and Bird Islands? Yes?___ No?___ Can't tell from the two clues.___ Explain your answer.

Third clue: People can go by plane between Bean and Bird Islands.

Use all three clues to answer Questions 2 and 3. Don't change your answer to Question 1.

Question 2: Can people go by plane between Fish and Bird Islands? Yes?___ No?___ Can't tell from the three clues.___ Explain your answer.

Question 3: Can people go by plane between Fish and Snail Islands? Yes?___ No?___ Can't tell from the three clues.___ Explain your answer.

The written responses were classified into the five Piagetian categories with the procedures detailed by Karplus and Karplus.[16]

Subject-Matter Examinations

Subject-matter examinations were constructed for biology, chemistry, and physics classes. These examinations tested understanding of the major concrete and formal concepts taught during the year. Each examination consisted of approximately fifteen concrete multiple-choice questions and fifteen formal multiple-choice questions. Sample items from those examinations are given below—the correct answer is preceded by an asterisk. One further point should be made concerning the concepts themselves. Specific definitions of concepts were necessary because most terms have more than one level of meaning or sophistication. This means that a term may be concrete or formal, depending on how it is defined or used in the students' text. An example is the biological term *niche*. Taken to mean an organism's profession, the term is a concrete concept. If, however, *niche* means an organism's trophic level, its spatial habitat, and its multidimensional hypervolume of environmental conditions of existence, it is clearly a formal concept.

Sample Questions

Biology Concrete Concept—Succession.

An area of ground was completely stripped of life by a fire. Six months later small grass-like plants were covering the ground. In two years small bushes had replaced the grass. After ten years poplar trees were covering the same area. Thirty years later the poplar trees were being crowded out by pine trees. This process is called:

[16]Karplus and Karplus, "Intellectual Development Beyond Elementary School I: Deductive Logic," *School Science and Mathematics,* (May, 1970), pp. 399–401.

A. the life cycle
B. biotic potential
C. ecological regression
*D. succession

Biology Formal Concept—Ecosystem.

In the early spring some chemical poison was dumped into a pond. It killed all the mold, bacteria, yeasts and other types of decomposers. By the end of the summer, members of the bass population of the pond began to die. The most likely reason for the bass deaths is:

A. The poison that killed the decomposers also killed the bass.
B. The bass had used the decomposers as a food source; since the food is no longer available the bass starved.
C. Bass ate the poisoned decomposers and poisoned themselves.
*D. The dead decomposers could no longer recycle nutrients so the productivity of the pond dropped to near zero.

Chemistry Concrete Concept—Extensive Properties.

Extensive properties of matter are properties that depend upon the amount of matter present. Which of the following is an extensive property?

A. color
B. boiling point
C. density
*D. length

Chemistry Formal Concept—Equilibrium.

Equilibrium defined for closed systems of liquids and gases is the state in which just as many molecules pass from liquid to gas as from gas to liquid; what would happen to the equilibrium condition if the closed container were doubled in volume?

*A. The number of molecules in the gaseous state would increase.
B. The number of molecules in the liquid state would increase.
C. The balance would not change since it was already at equilibrium.
D. The number of molecules in the entire system would double.

Physics Concrete Concept—Vector Addition.

Which of the following pairs of vectors has the resultant with the smallest magnitude?

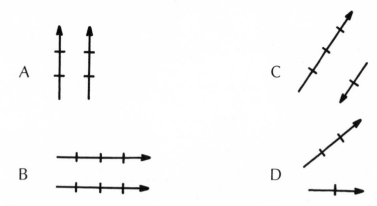

Physics Formal Concept—Stellar Parallax.

The relative observed position of some stars changes about $1/2500^\circ$ from January to July. The best explanation for this is:

A. The earth rotates on its axis.
*B. The observer moves.
C. The stars move.
D. Light rays from the stars bend.

Results

Operational levels of samples. To determine relative levels of intellectual development for the biology, chemistry, and physics classes, each subject was classified into one of seven categories on the basis of scores obtained during the individual interviews. The categories were: concrete-operational (IIA), transitional-concrete, concrete-operational (IIB), post concrete-operational, formal-operational (IIIA), transitional-formal, and formal-operational (IIIB).

The intermediate categories were considered appropriate and necessary because subject responses often were classified into different operational levels on different tasks. For example, responses of subject number 120 from the biology sample were classified concrete-operational (IIB) on the tasks conservation of weight, conservation of volume, and equilibrium in the balance. However, on the task separation of variables he demonstrated some beginning formal-operational thought, and here his response was classified IIIA. To classify this subject accurately, a category designated postconcrete-operational was created. Similar situations prompted the creation of other intermediate categories.

Figure 21 shows a comparison of means of the six tasks. It should be recalled that the tasks conservation of weight and conservation of volume had maximum scores of three and four, respectively. The tasks separation of variables and equilibrium in the balance showed very consistent means. This result indicates, as does comparison of individual raw scores, that the tasks are of approximately equal difficulty. However, the mean score of the ratio task is considerably higher, while the mean of the task islands puzzle is considerably lower. For that reason scores on the written tasks were determined to be unreliable determiners of formal thought, and scores from those tasks were not included in subsequent portions of the study.

Table 21 shows the number and percentage of subjects in each of the seven categories as classified on the basis of the four interview scores. Table 24 also shows that 29.5 per cent of the

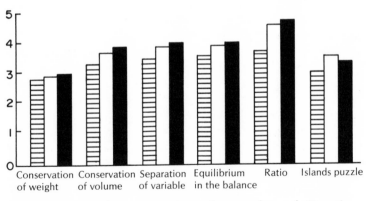

Fig. 21. Scores (left) in comparison of means for each Piagetian measure by task. The open columns represent the chemistry scores; the shaded columns, the biology scores; the black columns, the physics scores.

Subject	Concrete (IIA)	Transitional-concrete	Concrete (IIB)	Postconcrete	Formal (IIIA)	Transitional-formal	Formal (IIIB)
Biology							
Biology							
Number	3	6	6	18	17	1	...
Per cent	5.9	11.8	11.8	35.3	33.3	1.9	...
Chemistry							
Number	...	1	1	9	27	10	2
Per cent	...	2.0	2.0	18.0	54.0	20.0	4.0
Physics							
Number	...	1	...	11	9	8	4
Per cent	...	3.0	...	33.3	27.3	24.3	12.1

Table 24. Operational Levels of Biology, Chemistry, and Physics Samples

biology sample was determined to be fully concrete-operational, while an additional 35.3 per cent was postconcrete-operational. In effect 64.8 per cent of the sample was categorized as concrete-operational or part concrete-operational. Note that only one subject was categorized as transitional-formal, and no subjects were determined to be fully formal.

The chemistry sample shows most of the subjects somewhere in the transition between concrete (IIB) and formal ($IIIB$) thinking; 92 per cent of the sample was categorized as postconcrete, formal-operational ($IIIA$) or transitional-formal.

The physics sample also shows most of the subjects between concrete (IIB) and formal ($IIIB$); however, the percentage of fully formal subjects (12.1 per cent) is more than three times that of the chemistry sample. Still, a substantial portion of the sample (36.3 per cent) exhibited some concrete-operational characteristics (postconcrete or lower).

These samples are not necessarily representative of all biology, chemistry, and physics classes; therefore, generalizations must be made with reservations. It should be mentioned, however, that these results appear consistent with those reported in the literature cited earlier. The conclusion reached by other investigators—that a substantial portion of the high school population is operating on a concrete level—was supported. As expected, differences among biology, chemistry, and physics classes were obtained. A vast majority of the biology students were sophomores. Chemistry enrolls juniors and a few seniors, while physics enrolls seniors and very few juniors. This, plus the fact that physics and chemistry were electives and attract to a large extent only the educationally successful, explains the differences in the numbers of formal and concrete thinkers found in these classes.

Relationships with Concrete and formal-concept scores. The element of chance success on examination questions can be eliminated by using the formula

$$cp = \frac{kp - 1}{k - 1}$$

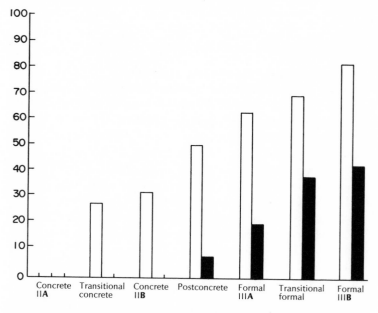

Fig. 22. A comparison of success on concrete and formal concepts with chance eliminated—pooled data. The open columns represent the concrete-concept questions; the black columns, the formal-concept questions.

where cp = corrected proportion of correct answers, p = obtained proportion, k = number of alternative answers to each item[17]

By use of this formula the adjusted percentage of correct responses for each of the seven operational-level categories was calculated. A comparison of success on concrete- and formal-concept questions with the element of chance eliminated is shown in Figure 22 for pooled data from the biology, chemistry, and physics samples. Data from each discipline are graphed separately in Figures 23 through 25.

In reference to the pooled data, note that the concrete-level

[17]J. P. Guilford, "The Determination of Item Difficulty When Chance Success Is a Factor," *Psychometrika*, Vol. 1 (1936), 259–64.

(IIA) subjects demonstrated no success on concrete or formal concepts. Also, no subject in the transitional-concrete and concrete level (IIB) demonstrated success above the chance level on formal concepts. This result supports the premise that

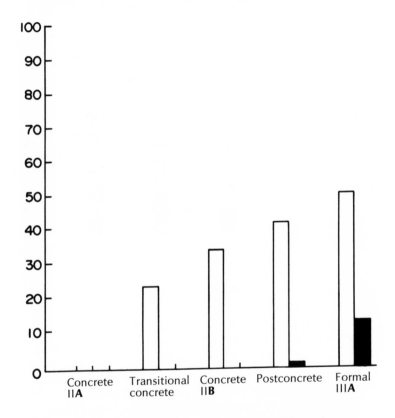

Fig. 23. Comparison of success on concrete and formal concepts with chance eliminated—biology. The open columns represent the concrete-concept questions; the black columns, the formal-concept questions. The column at the left represents the per cent of items answered correctly.

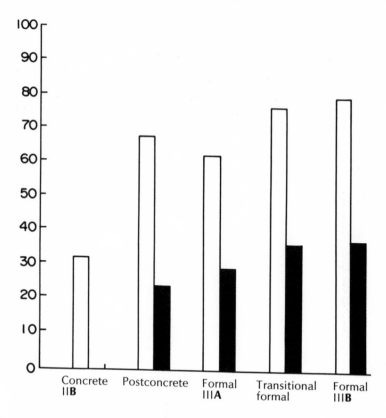

Fig. 24. Comparison of success on concrete and formal concepts with chance eliminated—chemistry. The open columns represent the concrete-concept questions; the black columns, the formal-concept questions.

concrete-operational subjects are unable to develop understanding of formal concepts. Further, support is demonstrated for the other major premises of the study: concrete-operational subjects are able to demonstrate understanding of concrete concepts, and formal-operational subjects are able to demonstrate understanding of both concrete and formal concepts.

The differences in mean scores of the seven operational categories of the pooled data were analyzed for significance through one-factor analysis of variance. Two analyses were performed. The first analysis tested for significant differences in the mean scores of the seven categories on the concrete-operational concepts, while the second tested for significant differences in the mean scores on formal-operational concepts.

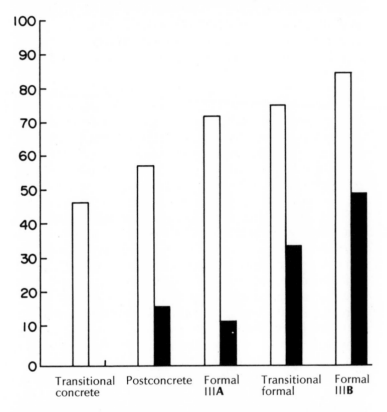

Fig. 25. Comparison of success on concrete and formal concepts with chance eliminated—physics. The open columns represent the concrete-concept questions; the black columns, the formal-concept questions.

The obtained F ratio for the difference in mean concrete-concept scores was 10.6752. This value exceeds the tabular value of 2.95 at the 0.01 level of confidence; therefore, it was concluded that these differences were significant.

The obtained F ratio for the difference in mean formal-concept scores was 8.8791. This value also exceeds the tabular value of 2.95 at the 0.01 level of confidence; therefore, it was concluded that these differences were also significant. Data plotted for each discipline separately show trends similar to the pooled data.

Multiple correlation coefficients. To analyze the degree of correlations between the Piagetian interview task scores and the concrete and formal examination scores, multiple-correlation coefficients were calculated. The coefficients were then tested for significance with an F test at the 0.05 and 0.01 levels of confidence. Table 25 shows the obtained multiple-correlation coefficients between the set of Piagetian interview task scores and the examination concept scores for each examination.

The multiple-correlation coefficients for the physics data were calculated without including the scores on the task conservation of volume. This was considered appropriate since that task was not designed to measure category $IIIB$ responses, while 88 per cent of the physics students demonstrated, on at least one occasion, this kind of response.

In all cases the multiple correlations are significant at the 0.05 level of confidence. In only two cases, the biology concrete items and chemistry concrete items, do the multiple correlations fail to reach significance at the 0.01 level of confidence. This result indicates two things: first, success on Piagetian tasks is significantly correlated with "understanding," as defined by the investigator; second, there appears to be a stronger correlation between the tasks and understanding of formal concepts than between the tasks and understanding of concrete concepts. Since the Piagetian tasks measure both levels of concrete and formal thinking, this result fits the Piagetian model.

Table 25. Multiple-Correlation Coefficients Between Piagetian Interview Task and Examination Concept Scores

Predicted Variable	Multiple Correlation Coefficient, R
Biology concrete-concept score	0.449*
Biology formal-concept score	0.592†
Chemistry concrete-concept score	0.458*
Chemistry formal-concept score	0.526†
Physics concrete-concept score	0.582†
Physics formal-concept score	0.541†

$^*p < 0.05;$ $^†p > 0.01.$

Semipartial-regression analysis. The multiple-correlation coefficients calculated for the previous six sets of variables were obtained in a stepwise fashion, as shown in Table 26. As each additional predictor variable was added to the regression equation, the value of the correlation between the predictor variables and the concept examination questions increased. For example, the calculated R for the task conservation of volume and the biology concrete-concept questions was 0.4141. When the next task, separation of variables, was added to the regression equation, the multiple-correlation coefficient increased to 0.4448. Inclusion of the task equilibrium in the balance further increased the correlation to 0.4491. From this example it is clear that the best single predictor is the task conservation of volume. The additional contribution of the next two tasks is relatively small, an increase in correlation of only 0.035.

The investigator asked these questions: (1) Is the increase in predictive power of using additional tasks large enough to

Predicted Variable	Predictor Variables	Stepwise Multiple Correlations	Beta Weights	Regression Constant
Biology concrete-concept score	Cons. of vol.	0.4141	0.2109	13.0822
	Sep. of var.	0.4448	-0.0791	
	Equil. in balance	0.4491	0.3583	
Biology formal-concept score	Cons. of vol.	0.4963	0.2795	-43.8856
	Equil. in balance	0.5609	0.2329	
	Sep. of var.	0.5919	0.2204	
Chemistry concrete-concept score	Sep. of var.	0.4552	-0.0203	9.8028
	Equil. in balance	0.4577	0.4452	
	Cons. of vol.	0.4580	0.0525	
Chemistry formal-concept score	Cons. of vol.	0.5098	-0.0459	38.5699
	Sep. of var.	0.5241	0.4788	
	Equil. in balance	0.5255	0.1388	
Physics concrete-concept score	Sep. of var.	0.5448	0.2318	35.3858
	Equil. in balance	0.5815	0.4332	
Physics formal-concept score	Sep. of var.	0.5114	0.4142	-4.9679
	Equil. in balance	0.5412	0.2019	

Table 26. Stepwise Multiple Correlation Coefficients, Beta Weights, and Constants for Regression Equations

justify using just one Piagetian task to predict student success on concrete- and formal-concepts examinations?

To answer the above, null hypotheses, that no significant increase in correlation occurs when additional variables are used, were tested for the preceding six sets of regression equations.

Table 27 shows the obtained F ratios for each of the six hypotheses tested. In each case the obtained F ratio was less than the corresponding table value at the 0.05 level of confidence. The null hypothesis that the additional variables do not add significantly in prediction of success on concept scores was, therefore, accepted in all six cases. This result was expected. The tasks are designed to measure only one thing, and a repetition of that measurement should add little in predictive power.

Table 27. Stepwise Multiple Regression, Best Single Predictors and Calculated F-Ratios

Predicted Variable	Best Single Predictor	df k, n-p-l	F ratio, Additional Predictors
Biology concrete-concept score	Cons. of vol.	2, 38	0.719
Biology formal-concept score	Cons. of vol.	2, 38	1.082
Chemistry concrete-concept score	Sep. of var.	2, 44	0.071
Chemistry formal-concept score	Cons. of vol.	2, 44	0.491
Physics concrete-concept score	Sep. of var.	1, 30	0.872
Physics formal-concept score	Sep. of var.	1, 30	3.176

Principle-components analysis. The statistical technique of principal-components analysis was used to determine the fac-

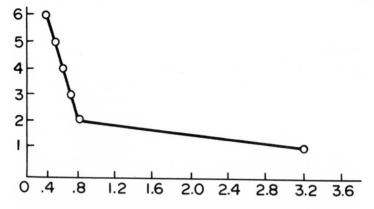

Fig. 26. Scree test for the number of factors. The horizontal figures represent the eigenvalues; the vertical figures, the ordinal numbers of the eigenvalue.

torial validity of the six Piagetian-styled tasks administered in this study. The scores on the Piagetian tasks from the three samples, biology, chemistry, and physics, were pooled and analyzed twice with use of program FACTOR. Pooling of the samples was appropriate since all six tasks were identical for each sample.

First, all components or roots were extracted, and, second, the program extracted only those components corresponding to eigenvalues of the correlation matrix that were greater than unity. Table 28 shows the results after a variance-maximizing rotation of the axes was carried out and only roots with values greater than one were extracted. Only one principal component was extracted, and this component accounts for 62.2 per cent of the variance of the sample scores. That percentage represents a relatively large portion of the variance.

When all roots are extracted and a Scree Test as shown in Figure 26 is used, a change in slope occurs between the first eigenvalue and the last five. This further indicates that only one factor represents a significant component of the six Piagetian tasks.

In reference once again to Table 28, note that tasks 2, 3, 4, and 5 correlate highly (0.84, 0.85, 0.80, and 0.80, respectively) with the first principal component. Tasks 1 and 6, conservation of weight and the islands puzzle, also load substantially (0.74 and 0.69 respectively) on this component. The task conservation of weight accounts for 55.49 per cent of its communality, or common-factor variance, and the islands puzzle accounts for 47.97 of its communality. Although these numbers are substantial, they are less than those for the other tasks, which range between 63.56 and 72.13 per cent.

Table 28. Principal-Components Analysis, Variance Maximizing Rotation

$(N = 134)$

Task	First Component Loading, 62.2 Per Cent of Variance	Per Cent Communality
1. Conservation of weight	0.74	55.49
2. Conservation of volume	0.84	70.40
3. Separation of variables	0.85	72.13
4. Equilibrium in the balance	0.80	63.56
5. Ratio	0.80	63.71
6. Islands puzzle	0.69	47.97

These results indicate that all the tasks, with the possible exception of conservation of weight and the islands puzzle, are measuring the same thing, namely formal-operational thinking. It will be recalled that the construct of formal-operational thinking and its regulation by what Piaget calls the "structured whole" represents a cornerstone of Piagetian theory. These results thus support the Piagetian constructs and factorially validate the formal-operational tasks.

Since the task conservation of weight was designed to measure concrete rather than formal thinking, its high correlation (0.74) with the first principal component was unexpected. A possible explanation is that only 10.4 per cent of the pooled sample was categorized IIA and scored 2 points, while 89.6 per cent was categorized IIB and awarded 3 points. Because of this, a very narrow range of highly skewed scores resulted, and the statistical analysis was not sensitive enough to extract the trend. To support this possible explanation, consider the biology sample, where 19.6 per cent of the subjects were categorized IIA. The task conservation of weight correlated less (0.59) in that group. Also, only 35.7 per cent of its communality was accounted for. This result indicates that the task may be measuring something other than formal thought (see Table 29).

Table 29. Principal-Components Analysis, Biology Sample, Variance Maximizing Rotation

$$(N = 51)$$

Task	First Component Loading, 55.5 Per Cent of Variance	Communality
Conservation of weight	0.59	35.77
Conservation of volume	0.76	58.16
Separation of variables	0.81	66.84
Equilibrium in the balance	0.74	55.91
Ratio	0.72	52.27
Islands puzzle	0.80	64.22

Conclusions and Recommendations

This investigation was carried out to find answers to the following questions: What are the levels of intellectual development of selected biology, chemistry, and physics students as determined by Piagetian tasks? What are the major concrete- and formal-operational concepts taught to those students? What are the relationships between students' scores on the Piagetian tasks and written test scores on concrete- and formal-operational concepts?

Conclusions. Data presented in Table 24 indicate that approximately 64.8 per cent of the biology students interviewed were operating entirely or partly at the concrete level. The chemistry subjects were best characterized as transitional thinkers, with 92 per cent of those interviewed categorized above concrete operational (IIB) and below fully formal-operational ($IIIB$). The physics sample also consisted largely of students operating somewhere between fully concrete- and fully formal-operational.

Approximately 85 per cent scored above concrete(IIB) and below formal ($IIIB$). Only 4.8 per cent of the entire sample of 134 students interviewed were judged to be fully formal thinkers ($IIIB$).

The results in Table 24 show that the vast majority of students in these classes were below the levels of intellectual development as outlined by Piaget. The investigator believes that some of the responsibility for this apparent "retarded" development can be traced directly to inappropriate subject matter and teaching procedures in today's schools. This point will be discussed further under "Recommendations."

Major concepts taught during the year in the respective classes were isolated and categorized as concrete or formal. This was a significant step in that such a classification scheme had not been attempted previously. Most of the concepts taught in the three science disciplines were categorized as formal.

On subject-matter tests that assessed the understandings of the major concrete and formal concepts in the respective disciplines of students in both the concrete and formal operational stages, the following results were obtained (see Figures 22 through 25). Subjects categorized as concrete operational (IIA)

demonstrated understanding of neither concrete- nor formal-operational concepts. Scores obtained on the subject-matter tests for these subjects, after correction for guessing, were zero for both categories of questions. Subjects categorized as transitional-concrete and concrete (II*B*) demonstrated understanding of approximately 30 per cent of the concrete-operational concepts, however, demonstrated no understanding of formal operational concepts. Of extreme significance is the finding that the understanding of formal concepts did not occur until at least some of the subjects' responses on the Piagetian tasks reached the level of formal operations. Not until the postconcrete category is any understanding of formal concepts apparent. This supports the premise that concrete-operational subjects are unable to develop understanding of formal concepts.

In reference once again to Figures 22 through 25, note that subjects in categories formal (III*A*), transitional-formal, and formal (III*B*) demonstrated understanding of both concrete and formal concepts. As the intellectual level increased, an increase occurred in the percentage of concrete- and formal-con-concept questions answered correctly. This increase in the percentage of formal-concept questions answered correctly is perfectly understandable in a Piagetian frame of reference. The increase in the percentage of concrete questions answered correctly from categories postconcrete to formal (III*B*) was not entirely expected. It was expected that, once a person had reached the highest level in concrete thought, any additional increase in intellectual development would make no contribution to the understanding of concrete concepts. The indication is, however, that formal thought does contribute to the understanding of concrete concepts. Two tentative explanations are offered for this finding:

1. Formal operations may help in the understanding of concrete concepts by the elucidation of a more comprehensive system of both concrete and formal content. This larger frame-of-content reference allows the learner to see relationships

involving concrete objects, situations, or events previously un-recognized. This expanded frame of reference thereby brings deeper meaning to concrete as well as formal content.

2. The teaching procedures used in the classrooms are largely expository; consequently, students seldom are confronted with firsthand concrete experiences with any aspects of the discipline. These procedures, in effect, render potentially concrete material abstract or formal, and the learner does not, therefore, have the opportunity to develop understanding of it until he enters the formal stage.

Analysis of the six Piagetian tasks used to assess levels of thinking with principal-components analysis showed the tasks to have factorial validity. All six tasks, including the conservation of weight, the two written tasks, the ratios task, and the islands puzzle, loaded substantially on the first principal component. Correlations between 0.69 and 0.85 were obtained, indicating that the tasks were measuring essentially the same psychological parameter. This result is significant in terms of Piagetian theory in that it supports Piaget's hypothesized construct of the unified nature of formal operations into the "structured whole."

The written tasks, however, were determined to be somewhat unreliable determiners of levels of thinking. Although these tasks presumably are measuring levels of intellectual development as defined by Piaget, scores on these tasks are often at considerable variance with those obtained during personal interviews. The ratios task, for example, seems to involve a simple proportion, the solution of which is probably attainable at the IIIA level of formal-operational thought rather than at the IIIB level as its authors indicate. Possibly the solution of this problem may also be obtained by the application of a previously memorized algorithm. Consequently, correct solutions may not demonstrate the acquisition of formal mental structures. Responses on the islands puzzle were often indicative of preoperational or concrete (IIA) operational thinking. This indeed was strange, in that some of the same subjects responded formally to the interview tasks.

Multiple-regression analysis of the four Piagetian interview-task scores and the concrete- and formal-concept scores indicated significant positive multiple correlations for each discipline.

Stepwise semipartial-regression analysis of the data indicated that the correlations between examination scores and the best single-predictor Piagetian task were not significantly increased by the addition of other Piagetian task scores to the regression equations.

These results indicate that, to obtain an initial indication of student levels of thinking, a teacher or investigator is justified in using a single Piagetian task. The task conservation of volume is relatively simple to administer, and the subject responses are extremely easy to categorize. For these reasons this task could serve as a practical initial indicator of student ability to operate with formal or abstract subject matter.

Recommendations. The results of this investigation indicate that a substantial portion of secondary school science subject matter is not suitable in terms of the intellectual level of the learner.

The biology sample investigated showed nearly 65 per cent of the students still largely at the concrete level of intellectual development. Since these students were found to be unable to develop an appreciable understanding of formal abstract concepts, it appears clear that for them a science course which deals with abstractions and "basic unifying themes" is highly inappropriate.

In the eagerness to update secondary school science programs during the 1960's one very important dimension apparently was left out—the learner. What is called for is a careful re-evaluation of the major content of these science courses in an attempt better to fit that content to the level of the learner. Perhaps more important than major shifts in content matter is a careful evaluation of teaching procedures and sequencing of materials to help lead the learners from concrete to formal thinking patterns.

Another possible alternative includes the use of curricular materials in the elementary and junior high schools that will confront students with firsthand experiences and real problems. Perhaps in this manner students will enter secondary science programs as formal thinkers able to comprehend the abstract nature of the courses. A further alternative involves the development of separate courses at the secondary level designed for only the concrete thinkers. This third alternative carries with it need for ability grouping, which has many drawbacks familiar to every educator.

Whichever direction schools choose to take, one thing is clear: the intellectual level of the learner must become a major consideration in curriculum reform.

10. What This Research Says to Schools

John W. Renner

From the beginning of this chapter the reader should keep firmly in mind that the impact that we feel our research has for schools does not confine itself to any one level. The first-grade learner can profit from this research, and so can the college student. The degree to which the research changes schools depends upon those in charge of them and the students in them. We have, therefore, divided this chapter into three parts — the impact this research has upon the classroom, the teacher, and the learner. These categories are not, of course, mutually exclusive, and at times in this chapter the lines dividing the categories are not perfectly clear.

The Classroom

Throughout the history of precollegiate education in the United States the public and the vast majority of the teachers have accepted the fact that educational environments in general and classrooms in particular have to be reasonably quiet if learning

174

is to go on. In fact, student interaction has been constantly discouraged throughout the schools. Detention halls, writing, "I will not talk in class," fifty to five hundred times, standing with nose against the chalkboard, putting tape over the mouth, and public rebuke are the kinds of punishment teachers have awarded students for talking in class.

It should be made clear that not all forms of student-to-student verbal interactions are being endorsed. Chemistry class need not be devoted to discussing the previous night's dates (although if something needs to be settled before the experiment can begin, perhaps it should be), and reading is not the time to argue about whose father has the fastest car. Generally, the interaction should be about the subject at hand, though there are exceptions to that statement.

It is important to look at the other side of social interaction. In an elementary school science class the group was doing an experiment with a rather bad-smelling chemical. One child smelled it and informed his classmates, "That stuff smells yukky!" Beautiful social interaction; everyone in the room understood him perfectly. As a reward for his succinct observation he was made to stand with his nose against the chalkboard. When the teacher was asked why she had awarded that punishment, she replied that "kids get out of hand if you don't really crack down on them." If she awards that particular punishment again, she will not do it in ignorance. The kind of social interaction we endorse was beautifully represented by the child's comment in science class.

Piaget is emphatic about the value of social interaction. He flatly states that the interaction of the learner with all phases of his environment represents one of four factors that assist a child in moving from one developmental level to the next (see Chapter 1). He goes further than human interaction; he emphasizes social *transmission*, which includes interaction with all phases of society—churches, schools, peer groups, and all other functions that are found in the milieu we call society. That, of course, says that the subjects a child studies and uses to move from stage to stage in the Piagetian model must be arranged to enable him to interact *directly* with the subject matter and not merely hear or read about it. That interaction often is with the physical objects of the discipline, as well as with those persons engaged in its study.

The classroom environment, then, must be one that encourages the students to interact with the discipline and each other *if* that environment is to reflect the Piagetian model. The research described in this book clearly demonstrates how establishing learning environments that encourage social interaction moves learners more deeply into the stages of Piaget's model. If, then, the development of the ability to think in abstract terms and to use propositional logic represents goals the school is pursuing, then the research cited here clearly demonstrates that the stereotyped, quiet, "tell 'em—show 'em—ask 'em," classroom is not the classroom that is needed. In every case the traditional classroom proved less effective than the one where inquiry was used to promote intellectual development. That finding alone makes the consideration of the Piagetian model by schools obligatory. Other data show that this environment promotes increased achievement on conventional standardized achievement tests.[1]

To implement a classroom environment that emphasizes social transmission, those persons working in the schools— *and particularly administrators*—must make a commitment to education that most do not now have. That commitment must be to the development of the intellectual capacities of the learner, and that development must be regarded as the *central* responsibility of the school. In the course of the research described in this book, a senior high school history teacher reported that he certainly hoped the elementary schools taught students to think because secondary schools did not have time

[1]John W. Renner, William J. Coffia, Don G. Stafford, Donald H. Kellogg, and M. C. Weber, "An Evaluation of the Science Curriculum Improvement Study," *School Science and Mathematics*, April, 1973, pp. 291–318.

When educational experiences are designed to teach the structure of the discipline and promote formal thought, the classroom often takes on a new definition.

to do that. "There is too much material to cover." That attitude cannot be held by a teacher or administrator who believes that the central responsibility of the school is the intellectual development of the student.

The use of the word "central" should not be misinterpreted. We use it exactly as the dictionary explains it—"in the center." Any time a teacher plans a learning activity, he must keep at its center the fact that that learning activity must contribute to the intellectual development of the learners. Even in teaching such skills as addition, spelling, and reading, the teacher must realize that central to those activities that make a contribution to intellectual development is the social transmission that can come from allowing children to work and study in pairs or groups. Transmission means moving from one point to another. Social transmission means, therefore, transmitting among points in the society. Since a society is composed of persons, social transmission means interacting with the persons around you. Schools are filled with young people of all sizes, ages, shapes, prejudices, beliefs, and backgrounds, but they form a society. Interacting with that society is difficult, at best, if the quiet classroom is what teachers and administrators demand.

The Teacher

The single most important commitment that must be made if intellectual development is to become the primary product of the schools—and the research reviewed in this book demonstrates that it can be—must come from the teacher. Before that, or at least simultaneously, the administrators must also have such a commitment. But when all philosophies have been agreed to and everything is in its proper place and perspective, the *teachers* in the classrooms are the ones who will determine whether intellectual development will be assisted or resisted. With respect to intellectual development, teachers represent the epitome of what Harry S. Truman meant when he said (discussing the presidency), "The buck stops here!" Teachers must make the basic decisions about what goes on in the classroom, and this research has shown that those activities are what hasten or retard intellectual development.

Before the teacher can assist students to develop intellectually, he must have made the decision that such assistance represents his responsibility. The job of teacher is not presently so viewed by most of those who have contact with and responsibilities in and for the schools. Presently most teachers believe that their principal role is the teaching of reading, American history, spelling, or some other subject. Some teachers in the elementary school are exceptions (the elementary teacher should be careful in so declaring himself; he must really understand what he believes), but most teachers are teachers of courses—subject matter. They are not generally interested in intellectual development and, if they recognize its importance at all, they equate it with the grades a student is awarded. Consider this view of courses:

A "course" generally consists of a series of briefings for the great Trivia contest. It's a kind of rigged quiz show. And it seems to work *only* if the participant values the "prize." The "prize," of course, is a "grade." An appropriate grade permits the participant to continue playing the Trivia game. All the while, let's not forget, very little, if any, substantive intellectual activity is going on.[2]

To say anything more would be belaboring the obvious. The research reported here makes abundantly clear that the traditional manner of presenting courses and evaluating those studying them does not promote much intellectual activity. That, of course, is the theoretical position of the authors of the foregoing quotation.

What does promote intellectual development? In Chapter 2 the research described utilized a program for the children in the experimental group that put materials into their hands and encouraged interaction between the materials and the children. Those children interacting moved more deeply into the concrete-operational stage and achieved greater reading readiness (Chapter 3) than did children not having such experiences. Those gains, to us, represent increased intellectual development. In Chapter 5 the experimental group outgained the control group in moving into the formal-operational stage. The junior high school students in that study also interacted with materials and other students in a manner not allowed the students in the control groups. Chapter 7 describes research at the college level, which again shows that social transmission promotes intellectual development.

A common thread winds all of this work together. Those

[2]Neil Postman and Charles Weingartner, *Teaching as a Subversive Activity* (New York, Delacorte Press, 1969), 152.

students who were involved in inquiring into the nature of what they were studying achieved intellectual development that was superior to those who did not have the experience. Two questions immediately arise: (1) What is inquiry? and (2) How does a teacher prepare student-content interaction to utilize inquiry?

Inquiry is the process used to find out something one does not know; the emphasis in that definition is on the word "process." To discuss inquiry beyond that point is beyond the scope of this book.[3] There are, however, several guidelines that teachers can profitably use in preparing a course that will be taught by inquiry.

Anyone qualified to teach a particular subject knows what concepts truly represent that subject. Furthermore, if that person is attuned to the needs and interests of learners, he will be able to select from his discipline representative ideas[4] that can be studied by the learners and will be valuable in promoting intellectual development. According to our research the isolation of the representative ideas of any discipline is the first step in preparing to teach in a way that will promote the greatest intellectual development—inquiry. *Any representative idea must be accurate* when judged from the discipline, but *it must also be capable of being inquired into.* A second-grade teacher, then, must select representative ideas for his mathematics class that represent good mathematics and that will

---

[3]For a thorough treatment of inquiry and its relationship to the classroom see Renner, Bibens, and Shepherd, *Guiding Learning in the Secondary School* (New York, Harper and Row, 1972); Renner and Stafford, *Teaching Science in the Secondary School*; John W. Renner, Gene D. Shepherd, and Robert F. Bibens, *Guiding Learning in the Elementary School* (New York, Harper and Row, 1973); Renner, Stafford, and Ragan, *Teaching Science in the Elementary School.*

[4]Philip H. Phenix states that, to overcome the surfeit of knowledge, a drastic process for its simplification must be found. To do this, he says, we must discover "for each discipline those seminal or key ideas that provide clues to the entire discipline." Phenix calls those key ideas representative ideas. See Philip H. Phenix, *Realms of Meaning* (New York, McGraw-Hill, 1964), 11.

In a classroom devoted to intellectual development the teacher often loses the traditional image.

also move the children deeper and deeper into the concrete-operational stage. Only when the teacher can make decisions about representative ideas is he qualified to select materials to use in the classroom. The teacher of American history, the art teacher — all teachers — must decide what representative ideas to teach because *those ideas become the concepts the learners develop.*

When the teacher has selected his representative ideas about fourth-grade science, United States government, or whatever, what does he do with them? As was said earlier, ideas must be not only representative but capable of being inquired into. Each of these ideas must be reachable by the learner through an investigation he conducts. That investigation begins with an *exploration,* which may include library research, science experiments, visits to various places where societal functions are carried on (such as a judicial court or a dairy), or any manner of things that will help the learner collect information about the representative idea being considered. After exploration the concept evolving from the representative idea is probably best understood by the learner if he *invents* it for himself, but there are times when the precise conceptual invention must be made by the teacher. Obviously, the intensive and extensive explorations that must be made before conceptual invention can take place must involve materials, and those materials must, of course, be selected; that is the second major selection task of the teacher.

The learner now has collected information and has invented (or has had invented for him) a concept that is now his representative idea about the discipline. That idea allows him to organize all he has found out during his explorations. The teacher has told him what materials are available for him to use, helped him when he was in need of help, asked him questions about what he was doing and why he was doing it a particular way, and, in general, guided him through the exploration and invention phases.

Next, the learner is provided the epitome of the social-transmission experience. The teacher gathers all the learners together, and they present evidence why they believe a particular idea is structured as it is. The emphasis during this phase of the learning is on *evidence*: How do you know that what you believe is really true? How could you prove or disprove your findings in another way? In other words, what *discoveries* can you make with the representative idea that could not have been made without it?

Exploration, invention, and discovery are the phases of inquiry, and they can be used to promote the equilibration and disequilibration that are necessary if children are to develop intellectually. The several curriculum vehicles used in the research discussed in this book provided experiences for the learner that led him to explore, invent, and discover, and increased intellectual development was the result of those experiences.

A teacher who is interested in promoting maximum intellectual growth among the learners in his classes can best exhibit that concern by the manner in which he organizes the learning experiences. A chart of the teacher's responsibilities and classroom procedures is shown below:

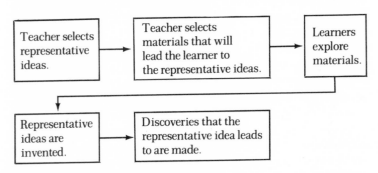

None of the foregoing will happen, however, unless the teacher in the classroom adopts the promotion of intellectual development as his primary responsibility. Our evidence tells us that not too many teachers have made that adoption.

The Learner

The reader has probably, at this point, developed a reliable feeling about the impact the research discussed in this book can have upon the learner. As he probably has concluded, separating the impact upon the learner from the other two categories in nearly impossible. There are, however, some unique implications the research has for the learner.

The research told us that organizing a series of learning experiences along lines that will push students deeper and deeper into a particular Piagetian level is no panacea. While all students profited from the experience, some learners were benefited more than others. In other words, a range of abilities was still evident in the classes, but the lowest point in the range was now higher than before. Individual differences remained.

The acceptance of the Piagetian levels concepts by the teacher can have a profound effect on the learner. To accept the Piagetian concept, one must accept his learning model, as well as his intellectual-development model (see Chapter 1). The acceptance of the latter gives the teacher an entirely new set of *expectations* with respect to what a learner can do. As one teacher told us about a second-grade child, "I always thought that child was lazy and that that is why he did not learn to subtract. Now that I know he cannot reverse his thinking, I no longer feel he doesn't want to learn to subtract. I know he can't." Understanding where learners are in the Piagetian developmental model can greatly alter a teacher's expectations of a particular child. Understanding of the model can also influence what a teacher expects from an entire class. A physics teacher whose students we were evaluating asked us to let him know if his class was not formal-operational, because he had assumed that they were, and if his assumption was incorrect, he would have to "change the way I am doing some things." The research, then, says a great deal to teachers about what they can expect from a learner.

The research described in Chapter 9 has enormous importance for the learner. Those findings clearly indicate that concrete-operational thinkers cannot develop understandings of formal-operational concepts. Perhaps we should temper that conclusion by stating that concrete-operational thinkers cannot develop understandings of formal concepts that can be measures with the instruments we designed. When those results are coupled with those of Chapter 6, which demonstrate that large percentages of the secondary population are concrete-operational, the secondary teacher acquires an important responsibility—he must be able to differentiate clearly between concrete and formal concepts. Furthermore, secondary teachers

Acceptance of the fact that many different kinds of experience are necessary to move children through the stages in the Piagetian model will alter what have been traditionally known as "school experiences."

must be able to identify the formal and concrete thinkers in their classes in order to adjust their own expectation levels when comparing a student's understanding of concepts with his intellectual level.

Perhaps the results of the research reported in Chapter 9 have greater implication for grades one through six than for any other level. The school years from kindergarten through sixth grade represent the time in a child's life when he develops understanding of the basic skills—reading, writing, and computation—and forms attitudes toward learning that he will probably carry the remainder of his life. Data show that children in those grade levels are concrete-operational thinkers.[5] In many areas of the country the middle-school concept is being implemented, and the grade levels in the middle school generally include the sixth. To check our hypothesis that sixth-graders are concrete thinkers, we interviewed a total of thirty-three sixth-graders—using the conservation-of-volume task that utilizes metal cylinders—who had been randomly selected from the classes in science in two middle schools, which consisted of grades six, seven, and eight. Six of the thirty-three (18 per cent) were rated as having entered the formal-thought stage—class III*A*. Four of the remaining twenty-seven students correctly explained the problem *after* the cylinders were submerged; as we stated in Chapter 4, that places the interviewee in class II*B*—late concrete operational. In other words, the thinking of twenty-seven of the thirty-three students interviewed (82 per cent) is still completely at the concrete-operational level. As has been said repeatedly in this book, such students must have concreteness to work with; they cannot comprehend formal-operational concepts, and requiring them to attempt to do so does not allow them the opportunities necessary to construct the mental structures they need to move into the stage of formal thought.

The research in Chapter 9, therefore, demonstrates that teachers need to develop their abilities to identify concrete and formal concepts and concrete and formal thinkers. The procedures used for concept identification are found in Chapter 9 and those for identification of formal thinkers, in Chapter 4. Before selecting tasks to use to identify formal thinkers, however, the teacher needs to study carefully the data and computation in Chapter 8. Those data provide a solid theoretical basis for selection.

---

[5]Renner, Brock, Heath, Laughlin, and Stevens, "Piaget Is Practical," *Science and Children*, Vol. 9, No. 2 (October, 1971), 23–26.

In our opinion, based upon observation of students at all levels during our research, the greatest impact the acceptance of the Piagetian model by a school and/or teacher can have on the learner is the opportunities provided him to individualize his own instruction. Earlier exploration, invention, and discovery were discussed as the procedures a teacher would use to involve a learner in studying a representative idea. During the time the learner is exploring, inventing, and discovering, he is working at his own pace and seeing those things which the situation suggests to him. He is not seeing the world through anyone else's eyes; he is his own man. He is working as fast as he wishes. He is, in other words, teaching himself. That is, we believe, the only defensible definition that can be given for "individualized instruction."

Much of what is called individualized instruction is simply breaking down into smaller and smaller pieces what adults want children to learn. That, incidentally, is also the major failing of programmed learning. But in exploration, invention, and discovery—inquiry—no one can direct the learner what to see in an object, an event, or a situation; *he* is the one who is involved, and *he* must make the decisions. To be sure, the teacher can direct a child to what to find in his explorations and what discoveries to make, but *that teacher does not believe in inquiry.* In addition, he does not believe in the learning model of Piaget, which says that experiences will have an impact on the development of the learner only if the learner himself is involved. To use Piaget's words, ". . . each time that we try to teach them something too quickly, we keep them from reinventing it themselves."[6]

In the section "The Classroom" above it was claimed that the results and implementation of the research described in this book would have a definite impact upon the freedom the learner has in the classroom. In order to explore, invent, and discover, he must have freedom. *Freedom does not imply license, how-*

[6]Piaget "Foreword" in Almy, *Young Children's Thinking,* iv.

ever. That is, the student does not have the license to do as he pleases. He can do as he pleases with the materials provided him that will lead him to the representative idea under consideration. The teacher must realize that such freedom means that occasionally the learner must just sit and think about what he is doing, has done, or will do. Too often when non-educators (and some educators as well) observe a classroom devoted to intellectual development, they see only the freedom of the learners and intuitively conclude that such freedom is noneducational. The research reported here can change the manner in which a student participates in his education. But it should be borne in mind that he *must* participate. In fact, if one word were selected that would describe why the results reported here were achieved, that word would be *participation.*

Epilogue

Embracing the results of the research reported in this book and implementing them would obviously affect the schools in many ways. Probably the most drastic necessary change would be the acceptance by schools of the responsibility for the intellectual development of students, rather than assuming that it exists and teaching accordingly. As evidence that schools and curriculum makers feel little responsibility for intellectual development, consider the following evaluation by Kohlberg and Gilligan of the mathematics, science (see Chapter 9), and social-studies curricula—all with the modifier "new"—that appeared in the senior high school in the late fifties and early sixties:

These curricula reforms were guided by the notion that more intellectual content could be put into high school and that this content should not be factual content and rote skills, but the basic pattern of thinking of the academic disciplines of mathematics, physics, or social science. The focus was to be upon understanding the basic logical assumptions and structure of the discipline and the use of these assumptions in reflective or critical thinking and problem-solving. *Clearly the new curricula assumed formal-operational thought rather than attempting to develop it.*[7]

According to the foregoing statement, secondary school science and mathematics ignore their responsibility for the intellectual development of students when curricula are designed and implemented. *That position says that all learners are capable of doing abstract thinking.*

The position just ascribed to educational practice reflects what we feel to be the basic ill of the educational enterprise— its lack of an adequate theoretical base. When instruction begins at the first grade in a formal vein and continues that way through a doctorate, the system is saying that all learners are alike. To be sure, that is a theoretical base, but it reflects a simplistic view of human learning. Education needs to establish firmly a theoretical base that can be used to educate teachers, select curricula, conduct classroom instruction, report to parents, build school buildings, and conduct all of the business of the discipline. No such base, in our opinion, now exists. If it did, the situation that Kohlberg and Gilligan referred to would not have developed.

The business of education is teaching the learner. *Any theoretical base, therefore, must include how the learner goes about learning and what he can learn as its center. That center, then, must guide, direct, and support all other activities and functions of the discipline.* Until education develops a sound theoretical base, it will not become a discipline with the stature of physics, English literature, or history. Rather it will subject to the whims and emotions of each education professor, school principal, and/or classroom teacher. If one doubts the power and importance of a theory base for a discipline, let him consult the condition of medicine before and after the establishment of the germ theory of disease.

[7]Kohlberg and Gilligan, "The Adolescent as Philosopher: The Discovery of the Self in a Postconventional World," *Daedalus*, Vol. 100, No. 4 (Fall, 1971), 1051–86. Italics added.

Our hypothesis is that Piaget's findings about learning and intellectual development constitute the building blocks from which a sound theory base for education can be constructed. To be sure, much more needs to be known. The research described here demonstrates that inquiry-oriented experiences in science at the elementary level, in the junior high school, and at the college level led learners to move from one intellectual level to another. The purpose of those curricula, however, was not to accelerate student movement through the stages of intellectual development; their purpose was to portray accurately and teach the discipline they represented. The fact that intellectual development occurred was a bonus. Would inquiry experiences in all disciplines produce similar results? Such questions as this and others must be answered before the Piagetian model can become a theory base for education. That model, however, deserves testing, and our belief is that, given the opportunity, it can become the theoretical base American education has needed since its beginning. The research described in this book demonstrates, we believe, that the utilization of the Piagetian model as a framework for an American educational-theory base can prove to be productive.

In addition to the foregoing, the impact of this research upon relationships with parents, building design, school furniture, the organization of libraries and media centers, music, athletics, all kinds of extracurricular programs (which may not in fact be "extra"), and in particular the books and other materials students use is potentially enormous. Imagine, for example, a mathematics program that recognizes the need to develop the intellectual capacities of students rather than assuming that formal-operational ability is present.

The time has come when the people who are paying for schools must make some demands on it. The research reported here leaves no doubt that intellectual development can be an outcome of education. Unfortunately, those in charge of schools do not often recognize it as important. A college dean recently described a student as a person who did not do abstract thinking at all well but was nevertheless a good student. Those two points of view would be incompatible *if* the Piagetian model became the theoretical base of education. The tragedy of the comment was that the dean did not recognize the absurdity of his position. Evidently there is much work to do.

Index